A Bevy
of Beasts

BY

Gerald Durrell

ILLUSTRATIONS BY

Edward Mortlemans

A TOUCHSTONE BOOK
Published by Simon and Schuster
New York

First Touchstone Edition, 1980
Published by Simon and Schuster
A Division of Gulf & Western Corporation
Simon & Schuster Building
Rockefeller Center
1230 Avenue of the Americas
New York, New York 10020
TOUCHSTONE and colophon are trademarks of Simon & Schuster.

Designed by IrvingPerkins
Manufactured in the United States of America

1 2 3 4 5 6 7 8 9 10
1 2 3 4 5 6 7 8 9 10 Pbk.
Library of Congress Cataloging in Publication Data
Durrell, Gerald Malcolm, date.
A bevy of beasts.

(A Touchstone book)
1. Zoo animals. 2. Zoological Society of
London. Gardens. Whipsnade Park. I. Title.
QL77.5.D87 1980   636.08′899′0924   80-15460

ISBN 0-671-21457-8
ISBN 0-671-41388-0 Pbk.

FOR BIANCA AND GRANDY,
IN MEMORY OF
THREE-QUARTERS OF A GORILLA
AND MANY OTHER THINGS

Contents

CHAPTER 1

A Bevy of Beasts

———◆———

He prayeth well, who loveth well
Both man and bird and beast.
—Coleridge, *The Ancient Mariner*

THEY say that a child who aspires to be an engine driver very rarely grows up to fill that role in life. If this is so, then I am an exceptionally lucky person, for at the age of two I made up my mind quite firmly and unequivocally that the only thing I wanted to do was study animals. Nothing else interested me.

I clung to this decision throughout my formative years with the tenacity of a limpet and drove my friends and relatives mad by catching or buying and inserting into the house every conceivable sort of creature, ranging from monkeys to the humble garden snail, from scorpions to eagle owls. Harassed by such a pageant of wildlife, my family comforted themselves with the thought that it was just a phase I was passing through and that I would soon grow out of it. But with each fresh acquisition my interest in animals quickened and deepened until, by my late teens, I knew without a shadow of a doubt what I wanted to be. Simply, I wanted to become a collector of animals for zoos and, later on—when I had made my fortune this way—to have a zoo of my own.

This did not seem to me to be a very wild or unreasonable

ambition, but the difficulty lay in how to achieve it. There were, unfortunately, no schools for incipient animal collectors, and none of the professional collectors then operating would take on anybody who had only unbounded enthusiasm and very little practical experience to offer. It was not enough, I decided, to be able to say that you had hand-reared baby hedgehogs or bred geckos in a biscuit tin; an animal collector must know at the drop of a hat how to get a stranglehold on a giraffe or sidestep a charging tiger. But it was exceedingly difficult to gain this sort of experience while living in a seaside town in England.

This had been brought home to me recently in a rather forcible manner. I had received a phone call from a boy I knew in the New Forest who possessed what he described as a baby Fallow deer that he was hand-rearing. He explained that as he was moving to a flat in Southampton he was unable to keep this most desirable pet. It was tame and house-trained, he said, and could be delivered to me within twenty-four hours or sooner by his father.

I was in a quandary. My mother, the only member of my family who could be remotely described as sympathetic to my interest in wildlife, was out, so I could not ask her how she would view the addition of a Fallow deer, however young, to my already extensive menagerie. Yet, there was the deer's owner clamoring for an immediate reply.

"My dad says we'll have to destroy it if you don't have it," he explained lugubriously.

That clinched it. I said I would be pleased to take delivery of the deer, whose name was Hortense, the following day.

When my mother returned from shopping I had my story all ready, a story that would have softened a heart of stone, much less such a susceptible one as my mother possessed. There was this poor little fawn, torn away from its mother, now under sentence of death unless we helped. How could we refuse? My mother, convinced by my description that the fawn was about the size of a small terrier, said that to allow it to be killed was unthinkable when we could (as I pointed out) keep it in a tiny corner of the garage.

"Of course we must have it," she said.

She then phoned the dairy and ordered an extra ten pints of milk a day to be delivered, being under the vague impression that growing deer needed a lot of milk.

Hortense arrived the following day in a horse box. As the deer was led out of this conveyance by its owner it became immediately obvious that, firstly, Hortense was unmistakably male, and, secondly, that he was some four years old, He had a pair of chocolate-colored horns edged with a forest of lethal spikes and he stood, in his elegant white-spotted coat, some three and a half feet high.

"But that's surely not a baby!" said my mother, aghast.

"Oh, yes, madam," said the boy's father hastily, "only a youngster. Lovely animal, tame as a dog."

Hortense rattled his horns up against the gate like a crackle of musketry and then leaned forward and delicately plucked one of Mother's prize chrysanthemums. Chewing it in a meditative sort of way, he surveyed us with limpid eyes. Hastily, before Mother could recover from the shock of meeting Hortense, I thanked the boy and his father profusely, grabbed the dog lead that was attached to Hortense's collar, and led him toward the garage. Not for anything would I confess to Mother that I, too, had imagined Hortense to be a tiny, heart-melting fawn. I had expended a large sum of money on a feeding bottle for what now turned out to be, if not Landseer's *Stag at Bay*, a very close approximation of it.

Followed by Mother, Hortense and I entered the garage where, before I could tie him up, he had evinced a deadly loathing for the wheelbarrow, which he attempted unsuccessfully to toss in the air. He eventually had to content himself with merely overturning it and disemboweling it on the ground. I tied him to the wall and hastily removed any gardening equipment that I thought was liable to incur his wrath.

"I do hope he's not going to be too fierce, dear," said my mother worriedly. "You know how Larry feels about fierce things."

I knew only too well how my elder brother felt about anything, fierce or otherwise, in the animal line, and I was only too delighted that he, together with my other brother and sister, happened to be out when Hortense arrived.

"Oh, he'll be all right when he settles down," I said. "He's just high-spirited."

At that moment Hortense decided that he did not like being left alone in the garage and so he charged the door. The whole garage rocked to its foundation.

"Perhaps he's hungry," said Mother, backing down the path.

"Yes, I expect that's it," I said. "Could you get him some carrots and some biscuits?"

Mother trotted off to procure the necessary deer-soothing foodstuffs while I went in to grapple with Hortense. He was delighted to see me again, as the sideways sweep of his horns catching me in the pit of the stomach showed me. However, I found that, like most deer, he was greatly addicted to being scratched round the base of his horns and I soon had him in

14

a semicomatose condition. Then, when a large packet of water biscuits and a couple of pounds of carrots arrived, he fell to assuage the hunger which his journey had given him.

While he was thus engaged I phoned up and ordered straw, hay and oats to be delivered. Then, when Hortense had finished his meal, I took him for a walk on the nearby golf links, where he behaved in the most exemplary fashion. When I got him back home he seemed more than happy to be bedded down in a corner of the garage on a pile of straw with some hay and crushed oats for his supper. I carefully padlocked the garage door and left him. I really felt, as I went to bed, that Hortense was settling down and would make not only a remarkably attractive pet but would give me the experience with larger animals that I so urgently desired.

The following morning I was awakened at about five o'clock by a curious noise which sounded as though somebody were dropping high-explosive bombs at regular intervals in the back garden. Deciding that this was impossible, I wondered what on earth it could be. I could tell by the slamming of doors and muttered curses that the rest of the family were wondering what it could be too. I leaned out of the window and surveyed the back garden. There, in the dawn light, I could see the garage rocking to and fro like a ship on a rough sea while Hortense demanded his breakfast by the simple expedient of charging the garage door. Hastily I rushed downstairs and, with an armful of hay and some crushed oats and carrots, pacified him.

"What," inquired my older brother at breakfast, fixing me with an unfriendly eye, "have you got locked in the garage?"

Before I could deny all knowledge of anything in the garage my mother rushed nervously to my defense.

"It's only a tiny little deer, dear," she said. "Have some more tea."

"It didn't sound tiny," said Larry. "It sounded more like Mr. Rochester's wife."

"It's so tame," my mother went on, "and it loves Gerry."

"Well, it's a good thing somebody does," said Larry. "All I say is keep the damned thing away from me. Life is difficult enough without having herds of caribou in the garden."

I was not popular that week. My marmoset had tried to climb into bed with Larry in the early morning and, on being repulsed, had bitten him in the ear; my magpies had uprooted a whole row of tomatoes carefully planted by my other brother, Leslie; and one of my grass snakes had escaped and been found by my sister Margo, with piercing screams, behind the sofa cushions. I was determined, therefore, that Hortense should be kept well away from the family. However, my hopes were short-lived.

It was one of those rare days you sometimes get in an English summer when the sun actually shines, and Mother, carried away by this phenomenon, had decided to have tea on the lawn. So when Hortense and I got back from our walk across the golf links we were treated to the sight of the family sitting in deck chairs grouped round a trolley on which reposed the accouterments of tea-making, sandwiches, a plumcake, and large bowls of raspberries and cream. Coming suddenly round the side of the house and finding my family thus arrayed took me aback. Not so Hortense, who with one glance took in the peaceful scene. He decided that between him and the safety of the garage lay a monstrous and probably dangerous enemy with four wheels—a tea trolley. There was only one thing he could do. Uttering a harsh bleat as a war cry, he lowered his head and charged, whipping his lead out of my fingers. He hit the trolley amidships, getting his horns tangled and showering tea things in all directions.

My family were completely trapped, for it is extraordinarily difficult, if not impossible, to leave a deck chair with alacrity even in moments of crisis. The result was that Mother was scalded with boiling tea, my sister was bespattered with cucumber sandwiches and Larry and Leslie received, in equal quantities, the raspberries and cream.

"It's the last straw!" roared Larry, flicking mashed raspberries from his trousers. "Get that bloody animal out of here, do you hear?"

"Now, now, dear! Language," said Mother pacifically. "It was an accident. The poor animal didn't mean it."

"Didn't mean it? Didn't mean it?" said Larry, his face suffused.

He pointed a quivering finger at Hortense, who, somewhat alarmed by the havoc he had created, was standing there demurely with the tea cloth hitched to his antlers like a wedding veil.

"You saw it deliberately charge the trolley, and you say it didn't mean it?"

"What I mean, dear," said Mother, flustered, "is that it didn't mean to put the raspberries on you."

"I dont care what it meant," said Larry vehemently, "I don't want to know what it meant. All I know is that Gerry must get rid of it. I will not have rampaging brutes like that around. Next time it might be one of us it attacks. Who the hell do you think I am? Buffalo Bill Cody?"

So, in spite of my pleas, Hortense was banished to a nearby farm, and with his departure vanished my only chance of experience with large animals in the home. It seemed there was only one thing for me to do—get a job in a zoo.

Having decided this, I sat down and wrote what seemed to me an extremely humble letter to the Zoological Society of London, which, in spite of the war, maintained the largest collection of living creatures ever assembled in one spot. Blissfully unaware of the enormity of my ambition, I outlined my plans for the future, hinted that I was just the sort of person they had always been longing to employ, and more or less asked them on what day I should take up my duties.

Normally, such a letter as this would have ended up where it deserved—in the wastepaper basket. But my luck was in, for it arrived on the desk of a most kindly and civilized man, one Geoffrey Vevers, then superintendent of London Zoo. I suppose something about the sheer audacity of my letter must have intrigued him, for, to my delight, he wrote and asked me to attend an interview in London. At the interview, spurred on by Geoffrey Vevers' gentle charm, I prattled on interminably about animals, animal collecting and owning my own zoo. A lesser man would have crushed my enthusiasm by pointing out the wild impracticability of my schemes, but Vevers listened with great patience and tact, commended my line of approach to the problem, and said that he would give the matter of my future some thought. I left him even more enthusiastic than before.

Some time later I received a courteous letter from him saying that unfortunately there were no vacancies for junior staff at London Zoo but that I could, if I cared to, have a position as student keeper at Whipsnade, the Zoological Society's country zoo. If he had written offering me a breeding pair of snow leopards I could not have been more delighted.

Within a few days, wildly excited, I set forth for Bedfordshire, taking with me two suitcases, one stuffed with old clothes and the other stuffed with books on natural history and innumerable fat notebooks in which I was going to note down everything that I observed about my animal charges and record every pearl of wisdom that dropped from the lips of my fellow workers.

It was in the middle 1800s that the great German animal dealer Karl Hagenbeck created an entirely new form of zoological garden. Up until then animals had been stuffed into ill-designed, unsanitary, heavily barred cages that made it difficult for the public to see the animals and difficult for the animals to survive these appalling concentration-camp-like conditions. Hagenbeck had an absolutely new conception of how animals should be displayed. Instead of the grim, iron-barred dungeons, he gave his animals light and space, with huge artificial mountains of rocks to climb on, and he separated them from the public with either dry moats or moats filled with water. To the pundits of zoo keeping this was heresy. To begin with, they said it was unsafe, for animals were sure to get out of moats, and even if this did not happen, all the animals would die, for it was well known that unless you kept tropical animals in foggy, germ-infested steam heat they would die instantly. The fact that tropical animals frequently languished and died in these Turkish-bath-like conditions anyway was neither here nor there. But, to the pundits' surprise, Hagenbeck's animals flourished. They not only improved their condition in their outdoor quarters but even bred successfully. Once Hagenbeck had proved his contention that keeping animals under these conditions made them not only happier and healthier but a better and more spectacular show from the public's point of view, all zoological gardens in the world started to turn over to this new method of keeping and displaying their collections.

Whipsnade, then, was really London Zoo's attempt to out-Hagenbeck Hagenbeck. This huge farm estate perched up on the Dunstable Downs, some thirty miles north of London, had been purchased by the Society and laid out at considerable expense. Here animals were to be displayed in as close to natural surroundings as possible—that is, surroundings that to the anthropomorphic zoo-going public *seemed* natural. Lions were to have forests to live in; wolves to have woods; and for the antelopes and other hoofed animals, great rolling paddocks. From my point of view Whipsnade was the nearest approach to going on safari that one could attempt at that time. For this was in the days before the aristocracy of England were forced by crippling death duties to become a collection of zoo keepers.

Whipsnade, I found, was an extremely small village consisting of one pub and just a handful of cottages scattered lazily among valleys full of hazel copses. I went to the pay box to explain my presence and then, leaving my suitcases there, I went along to the administration building. Peacocks gleamed and shimmered as they dragged their tails across the green lawns, and in the pine trees along the main drive there hung a gigantic nest—like a haystack of twigs—around which Quaker parakeets chittered and screamed.

I went into the administration building and was then

ushered into the office of Captain Beale, the superintendent. He was sitting there in his shirtsleeves, sporting some very handsome striped braces. The large desk in front of him was piled high with a great assortment of papers, most of which looked terribly official and scientific, and a mound of them partially covered the telephone. As the captain stood up I saw that he was a man of immense height and girth, and he looked, with his bald head, steel-rimmed spectacles, his mouth drawn down into what was almost a sneer, exactly like one of the drawings of Billy Bunter. He came lumbering round the desk and stared at me, breathing heavily through his nose.

"Durrell?" he boomed interrogatively. "Durrell?"

He had a very deep voice and he spoke in a sort of muted roar which some people get into the habit of doing after many years on the West Coast of Africa.

"Yes, sir," I said.

"Glad to meet you. Sit down," said the captain. He shook my hand and retired behind his desk.

He threw his bulk back in the chair and it creaked alarmingly. He stuck his thumbs under his braces and played a tattoo on them with his fingers, staring at me. The silence seemed interminable. I sat timidly on the edge of my chair; I desperately wanted to make a good impression to begin with.

"Think you'll like it here?" said Captain Beale so suddenly and so loudly that I jumped.

"Er . . . yes, sir, I'm sure I shall," I said.

"You've never done any of this sort of work before?" he inquired.

"No, sir," I replied, "but I've kept a lot of animals at one time or another."

"Ha!" he said, almost sneeringly. "Guinea pigs, rabbits,

21

goldfish—that sort of thing. Well, you'll find it a bit different here."

I was longing to tell him that I had kept considerably more exotic pets than rabbits, guinea pigs and goldfish, but I did not feel that this was the right moment.

"I'll hand you over to Phil Bates now," boomed the captain, polishing his bald head with one hand. "He's the head keeper. He'll fix you up. I don't know where they're going to put you, but he'll find room for you on one of the sections."

"Thank you very much," I said.

He surged to his feet and waddled out of the office, and I followed him. It was rather like following in the footsteps of a mastodon. He scrunched out onto the gravel path and paused, glaring around him, listening.

"Phil!" he bellowed suddenly. "Phil! Where are you?"

So enormous and fierce was his voice that a peacock that had been busily displaying to itself gave him a terrified look, put down its tail and scuttled away as fast as it could.

"Phil!" roared the captain again. "Phil!"

Distantly, I could hear somebody whistling tunelessly. The captain cocked his head on one side.

"There he is," he said, "the bloody man! Why doesn't he come?"

Just at that moment Phil Bates, still whistling, slouched unhurriedly round the corner of the administration building. He was a tall, well-built man with a brown, kindly face.

"Were you calling me, Captain?" he asked.

"Yes," rumbled the captain. "Want you to meet Durrell here."

"Ah," said Phil, smiling at me, "Welcome to Whipsnade."

"Well, I'll leave you, then, Durrell," said Captain Beale. "You're in good hands with Phil. Er, see you around, I expect."

He flipped his braces with a sound like a cracking whip, bobbed his big, shining bald head at me and lumbered off back into his office.

Phil smiled affectionately at the captain's retreating back and then turned to me.

"Well," he said, "the first thing is to fix you up with some digs. I've had a word with Charlie Bailey about you—he's on elephants—and he seems to think that he can put you up in his cottage. Let's go have a word with him."

As we walked down the broad main drive there seemed to be peacocks everywhere flaunting their metallic tails at us, and golden pheasants, looking as though they had been constructed out of cheap Woolworth's jewelry, glowed in the undergrowth. Phil whistled tunelessly and happily to himself. It was, I discovered, a habit he had and you could always tell in which part of the grounds he happened to be by this incessant, tuneless whistle. Presently we came to a series of what looked like immense and very ugly pillboxes. These, I was to discover, formed the Elephant House. Behind them was a small shed in which all the elephant keepers were having their tea break.

"Er, Charlie," called Phil apologetically, "can you spare a minute?"

A short, stocky little man appeared, with a bald head and shy, rather dreamy blue eyes.

"Um, Charlie, this is, er—what's your Christian name?" asked Phil.

"Gerry," I said.

23

"This is Gerry."

"Hello, Gerry," said Charlie, smiling at me as though I was the one person he had always wanted to meet.

"Now, do you think you can find room for him in your cottage?" asked Phil.

Charlie smiled at me sweetly.

"I'm sure we can," he said. "I've talked it over with Mrs. Bailey and she seems to think it will be all right. Perhaps Gerry would like to go and see her?"

"Yes, that's a good idea," said Phil.

"How do I get there?" I asked.

"I'll show you," said Phil. "Come with me."

"See you later then, lad," said Charlie.

Phil led me out to the main gate and up to the edge of the common.

"Take that path over there and it's the first cottage on the left," he said, pointing. "You can't miss it."

I made my way down the path over the common, where the goldfinches were pinking and flashing scarlet and yellow among the newly budding gorse. At the top of the upper slope I came to the cottage, and I opened the gate and walked down through the little flower-filled garden and knocked on the front door. It was extremely peaceful; the bees hummed drowsily among the flowers; somewhere a wood pigeon was cooing self-satisfiedly to himself, and distantly came the yapping of a dog.

The front door was opened by Mrs. Bailey. She was a handsome woman with fine eyes; her hair was beautifully coiffured and her overall was spotless. She had the brisk, clean appearance of a hospital matron.

"Yes?" she inquired cautiously.

"Good morning," I said. "Mrs. Bailey?"

"Yes," she said, "that's me."

"Well, Charlie told me to come and see you. I'm Gerry Durrell. I'm new here."

"Oh, yes," she said, touching her hair and smoothing her apron. "Yes, yes, of course. Do come in."

She ushered me through a small hall and into a spotless parlor where there was a big kitchen range, a scrubbed table and comfortable, rather battered chairs.

"Do sit down," she said. "Would you like a cup of tea?"

"I'd love a cup of tea, if it's no trouble," I said.

"No trouble at all," she said earnestly. "How about a piece of cake or some scones? I've got some scones. Or would you like some sandwiches? I could make you some sandwiches."

"Well, I—I don't want to put you to all that trouble," I said, rather taken aback by this sudden largesse of food.

"Oh, it's no trouble at all," she said. "I know what you young men are like—always hungry. And anyway it's teatime. I won't be a minute; I'll just put the kettle on."

She bustled out into what was presumably the pantry and I heard her clattering crockery and plates around. Presently she reappeared and laid the table. In the center she placed an enormous plumcake, a whole pile of scones, a loaf of brown bread, a great pat of buttercup-yellow butter, and a pot of strawberry jam.

"The jam's homemade," she said.

She sat down opposite me.

"Tea won't be a minute. The kettle will be boiling in a second. Now just you tuck in and have something to eat."

She watched me indulgently as I helped myself to bread and butter and an enormous helping of strawberry jam.

25

"That's right," she said. "Now, what have you come to see me for?"

"Didn't Charlie explain?" I asked.

"Explain?" she said, cocking her head on one side. "Explain what?"

"Well, he said there might be a chance that you'd be able to find room for me to live here," I said.

"But I thought that was all settled," said Mrs. Bailey.

"Oh, is it?" I said, surprised.

"Yes," she said, "I said to Charlie, I said—and I trust his judgment—I said to Charlie, I said, you have a look at the boy and if you like him then he can come."

"Well, that's very kind of you," I said. "Charlie didn't tell me that."

"Reeely!" she said, "Reeely! Someday he'll forget his own head. I said I was perfectly willing to have you providing you were respectable."

"Well, I don't know about being respectable," I said doubtfully, "but I'll try not to be a nuisance."

"Oh, you won't be a nuisance." she said. "Well, *that's* all right, then. Where are your things?"

"I'll bring them down from the zoo later," I said.

"Good. Now that's settled I'll go and make some tea. Help yourself to some more bread."

"Er, there's just one more thing," I said.

"What's that?" she inquired.

"Well . . . Well, what do I have to pay you a week? You see, I don't get a very big salary and I can't afford very much, I'm afraid."

"Now," she said, wagging a finger at me sternly, "I don't want to rob you. I know what sort of salary you're going to get and I don't want to rob you at all. What do you suggest?"

"Would you say that two pounds would be too little?" I asked hopefully, thinking to myself that this would leave me one pound ten to buy cigarettes and other essentials of life with.

"Two pounds?" she said, shocked. "Two pounds? That's far too much. I said I wasn't going to rob you."

"But there's all the food and stuff to buy," I said.

"Yes, but I'm not robbing you to the tune of two pounds. Not me. You'll pay me twenty-five shillings a week. That's quite sufficient."

"Are you sure you can manage on that?" I asked.

"Of *course* we'll manage," she said. "I'm not having it said that Mrs. Bailey took advantage of a young man, especially when he's just started work."

"Well, I still think it's awfully little," I protested.

"Take it or leave it," she said, "Take it or leave it. You can go elsewhere if you like." She smiled at me and pushed the cake and scones nearer.

"Not if you make homemade strawberry jam," I said. "I'd rather stay here."

She beamed at me. "Good," she said. "We've got a nice little bedroom for you upstairs; I'll show it to you in a minute. Now I'll just make the tea."

Over tea she explained to me how Charlie normally worked at London Zoo but during the war he had had to be evacuated with the elephants to Whipsnade and so she had come with him. Elephants are single-minded creatures, and once they have accepted a keeper he generally has to remain with them for the rest of his life.

"We've got ever such a nice house of our own in Golders

Green," she said. "It really is spotless. It's very, very nice and although I says it myself as shouldn't, it's a credit to us both. Of course, this cottage is all right—it's quite comfortable here —but I shall be glad to get back to my own place. Besides, you know what people are, you can't always trust them. The last time I went up to have a look nobody had thought to scrub the front doorstep for ages. It was almost black. I could have cried. No, I shall be glad to get back among my own things, although it's been reely quite pleasant here in the country, I must admit."

After I had consumed several cups of tea, two slices of cake and vast quantities of strawberry jam and bread, Mrs. Bailey reluctantly removed the things from the table.

"Now, are you sure you've had enough?" she said, looking at me searchingly, as though trying to find signs of malnutrition on my face. "Are you quite sure you wouldn't like another slice of bread or another slice of cake or anything? And you haven't touched the scones!"

"No, really, honestly," I protested, "I couldn't eat any more or I'll never eat any supper."

"Ah, yes, supper," she said, and her face clouded. "Supper. I'm afraid I'll have to do something cold for supper. I hope you don't mind."

"No, I don't mind," I said.

"Well," she said, "you go up and find Charlie and then come back with him when he knocks off. Bring your things and we'll settle you in. How's that?"

So I made my way back over the common and up to the zoo. Here I wandered enraptured for an hour or so. Whipsnade was so vast I could not possibly explore all of it in the time, but I found the wolves' wood where the pine trees grew straight and close together, and in the gloom among their roots the wolves prowled with sly eyes, slinking from tree to tree and occasionally having yapping, yarring fights with each other. They moved so rapidly and silently through the trees that it was like watching flakes of wood ash caught on sudden eddies of wind. Near to the wolves an acre or so of ground had been enclosed for the brown bears—great bum-

bling, biscuit-colored ones that meandered and snuffled and dug with their claws in amongst bramble and gorse bushes that grew in their enclosure.

I was entranced at seeing animals under these conditions. To me it seemed the ideal way to keep them. I had yet to learn that a very large area to keep animals in is a mixed blessing both from the animal's and the keeper's point of view.

Suddenly I remembered the time and I hurried back to the Elephant House and met Charlie. We picked up my suitcases and made our way across the common to the cottage.

"Take your boots off, both of you" said Mrs. Bailey as she opened the door to us. "I don't want mud over my nice clean floors."

She pointed to where she had spread newspaper in the hall. Dutifully we took off our boots and went in stockinged feet into the parlor where the table was groaning with food—ham, tongue and salad, new potatoes, peas, beans, carrots, and an enormous trifle wearing an ample coat of cream.

"Now, I'm not sure whether there's going to be enough," said Mrs. Bailey worriedly. "It's only a snack, I'm afraid, but it'll have to do."

"It looks all right to me, dear," said Charlie, in his soft voice.

"Well, it's not quite what I had in mind. The boy needs something hot. But anyway it'll have to do."

We sat down and started to eat. The food was delicious and we ate in companionable silence for a while.

"What made you come to Whipsnade, Gerry?" asked Charlie at last, dissecting his plateful of food with gentle thoroughness.

"Well," I said, "I've always been interested in animals and I want to become an animal collector—you know, go out to

Africa and places like that and bring animals back for zoos. I want to get experience with some of the bigger things. You know, you can't keep big things down in Bournemouth. I mean you can't have a herd of deer in a suburban garden, can you?"

"Ah," he said, "no, I see that."

"Have a little more salad," said Mrs. Bailey, oblivious to the difficulties of keeping big game in a back garden.

"No, I've got plenty here," I said, "thanks."

"So when are you going to set off?" asked Charlie. He was quite serious. I warmed to him.

"Well, as soon as I'm trained," I said.

Charlie nodded and then smiled secretly and gently to himself, his lips moving soundlessly. This was a habit he had, of smiling and silently repeating to himself what you had just said to him, as though to memorize it.

"Finish up these peas," said Mrs. Bailey. "They'll only be thrown away."

Eventually, replete with food, we made our way upstairs to bed. My room was an oak-beamed one lying under the eaves of the cottage. It was comfortably furnished and by the time I had finished unpacking my books and clothes it looked to me positively palatial. I climbed into bed and heaved a great sigh of triumph. I had arrived. I was there—at Whipsnade. Gloating over this thought, I fell asleep, to be awakened—it seemed—only seconds later by Charlie bringing me in a cup of tea.

"Up you get, Gerry," he said. "Time for work."

After a crisp and sizzling breakfast of sausages, bacon and eggs, and a large pot of tea, Charlie and I made our way over the dew-blurred common and in through the gates of the park together with a milling crowd of fellow workers.

31

"Where are you working, Gerry?" inquired Charlie.

"I don't know," I said. "Phil Bates didn't tell me."

Just at that moment Phil Bates appeared at my elbow.

"Ah," he said, "good morning. Settled in? Good."

"Where do you want me to work?" I inquired.

"I thought," said Phil judiciously, "I thought that this morning you could start on the lions."

CHAPTER 2

A Lusk
of Lions

For lo, the gentil kind of the lioun! ..
—CHAUCER, *The Legend of Good Women*

I ADMIT it came as something of a shock to be told that I was to start work on the lions. I flatter myself that I showed no outward sign of uneasiness when Phil told me, but I did feel he might have let me start on something fairly tame—a herd of dewy-eyed deer, for example. It seemed rather unfair to pitchfork me in amongst a lot of lions before I had got to grips with the job. However, I received the news with all the nonchalance I could muster and set off through the park in search of my section.

I found that the section was spread out along the crest of the Downs, half hidden in a fringe of elder bushes and tall nettles. Where the hillside dropped down to the valley this undergrowth ended and its place was taken by great cushions of green grass, each harboring an ants' nest under its rabbit-cropped wig. From this point there was a magnificent view over the mosaic work of fields that separated you in a broad sweep from the downland across the valley, fields whose pastel colors seemed to shift and change as the great cloud shadows swept across them.

The nerve center of the section was a small, tumbledown hut hemmed in a copse of tangled elder bushes. The hut wore a toupee of honeysuckle at a rakish angle, practically obscuring one of its two windows and so making the interior dark and gloomy. Outside it sported a battered notice board on which was the euphemistic title "The Haven." The furnishings were monastic in their simplicity—three chairs in various stages of decay, a table that rocked and jumped like a nervous horse when anything was placed on it, and a grotesque black stove that crouched in one corner pouting smoke through its iron teeth and regurgitating embers in quite incredible quantities.

It was in this dim hutch that I discovered the two keepers who were in charge of the section. Jesse was a red-faced, taciturn individual with fierce blue eyes under shaggy white brows and a nose the color and texture of a large strawberry. Joe, on the other hand, was brown-faced and, with his twinkling blue eyes and husky, infectious laugh, he exuded good humor. When they had finished their breakfast, which my arrival had interrupted, Jesse walked the length of the section with me, showing the animals and explaining the work. At one end of the section there was the wombat, Peter, then an enclosure full of arctic foxes and another full of raccoonlike dogs. Then came the cage containing the two puffball-white polar bears and a pit containing one pair of tigers. Farther along the Downs was a great enclosure in which there was another pair of tigers and then, finally, the animals from which the section took its name, the lions.

We walked along the narrow, twisting path through the elder bushes and came eventually to the tall barred fence that surrounded the lions' cage. This was some two acres in extent, built on the slope of the hill and thickly overgrown with bushes and trees. Moving along the barrier rail, Jesse and I came to a spot where this undergrowth curved back to form a dell, and here an area of long, lush grass surrounded a pool. Lying there, grouped picturesquely under a gnarled and twisted thorn tree, lay the lions. Albert, the male, lay in the pale sunlight, wrapped up in his mane, meditating. Beside him lay Nan and Jill, his golden, butter-fat wives, both fast asleep, their soup-plate paws twitching gently. Jesse shouted their names and rattled a stick along the wire, wanting them to come over and be introduced. Albert merely turned his head for a brief moment, gave us a withering look and returned to his meditations; Nan and Jill did not even stir. They did not look fierce and wild to me; in fact, they looked overweight, lazy and slightly superior. Jesse took up a stance with his feet apart as though on the deck of a rolling ship, sucked his teeth vigorously and fixed me with his fierce blue stare.

"Now, you listen on me, son," he said. "You listen on me and you won't go wrong. That there wombath, them foxes and them raccoons, you can go in with them, see? But don't you try no tricks with these others or they'll have you. They may looks tame, but they're not, see?"

He sucked his teeth again and surveyed me to see whether I had absorbed this lesson. I assured him that I had not the slightest intention of taking any chances with anything until I had got to know them. I felt—but did not say so—that it would be rather infra dig to be eaten by a tiger that you had not, so to speak, been introduced to.

"Well, you listen on me, son," said Jesse again, nodding portentously, "and I'll learn you."

My first few days were fully occupied with the learning process, memorizing the routine work of feeding, cleaning and other daily chores, but this routine work was fairly basic, and once I had mastered it I had more opportunity for watching the animals in our care and trying to learn something about them. Both Jesse and Joe were vastly amused at the fact that I carried an enormous notebook in my pocket and would at the slightest provocation whip it out and make an entry.

"Bloody Sherlock Holmes," was Jesse's description of me, "always writing frigging things down."

Joe would attempt to pull my leg by describing long and complicated actions that he had just seen the animal performing, but he would always let his imagination get the better of him and I could spot the deception.

Naturally enough, I started my researches on the lions. Being for the first time in my life on an intimate footing with these beasts, I decided to read up all I could about them and see how it tallied with my own observations. I discovered, not altogether to my surprise, that there is probably no other animal (except some purely mythological creatures) that has been endowed with so many imaginary virtues. Ever since someone in a moment of unzoological enthusiasm named it the King of the Beasts, writers have vied with each other to produce proof of the lion's right to this title. This particularly applied, I found, to the ancient writers, who were unanimous in praising *Felix leo* for its sweetness of character, sagacity, courage and sportsmanship; thus, I suppose, it was a foregone conclusion that it should be adopted as a national emblem by that modest and retiring race, the English. I had not been working with Albert and his wives for any length of time before I discovered that lions were not all that the old writers cracked them up to be.

In a translation of Pliny's *Natural History* published round about 1674, I found the following delightful account of the King of the Beasts:

> The Lion alone of all wild beasts is gentle to those who humble themselves unto him, and will not touch any such upon their submission, but spareth what creatures soever lieth prostrate before him. As fell and furious as hee is otherwhiles, yet hee dischargeth his rage upon man, before that hee setteth upon women, and never preyeth upon babes unlesse it be for extreme hunger.

After knowing Albert for only three days I realized that this description did not fit him. He was, to be sure, as fell and furious as he could possibly be, but I do not think he had an ounce of mercy in his makeup. Anyone who had attempted to lie prostrate in front of him would have received a bite in the back of the neck for his pains.

Another old writer I perused was Samuel Purchas, and he informed me, with all the assurance of one who has never seen a lion, that "the Lyons in cold places are more gentle, and in hotter more fierce." When I first read this it gave me a certain hope that I would be able to get on friendly terms with Albert, for just after my arrival at Whipsnade the weather had turned cold and an icy wind roared across the Downs, making the misshapen elder bushes creak and groan and shudder against each other. In this type of weather, according to Purchas, Albert and his wives should be gamboling around like friendly kittens.

On my second morning my faith in Purchas was rudely shattered. I was walking past the lions' cage, bent double against the wind and blue with cold, on my way back to the shelter and warmth of The Haven. Albert had concealed himself in a thick bed of grass and nettles in the curve of the cage near the path. He had, I am sure, seen me pass earlier and had decided that he would surprise me on my return journey. He waited until I was opposite and then he suddenly jumped out against the bars with a hair-raising cough of wrath. Then he squatted on his haunches and glared at me, his yellow eyes full of ferocious amusement at my sudden panic. He decided that this was a good joke and repeated it later the same day. Again he had the pleasure of watching me leap in the air like a startled stag, but this time he was gratified to observe me drop the bucket I was carrying, trip over it, and fall heavily into a bed of particularly luxuriant nettles. I discovered afterward that cold weather, instead of making Albert gentle, infected him with a dreadful skittishness, and he would spend his time hiding behind bushes and leaping out at unsuspecting old ladies as they passed. I presume that this exercise increased his circulation when there was a nip in the air.

I continued to read Pliny and Purchas on lions, but with a more discriminating eye. After a hectic day being jumped out at by Albert I found that their lions had a nice, soothing fairy-tale quality about them that made them much more endearing than the real lions I was looking after. I particularly liked the travelers' stories of their meetings with lions in the wilds, all of which underlined the intelligence and sweetness of the animals' character. Pliny relates how Mentor the Syracusan met a lion in Syria that appeared to be irresistibly drawn to him, bouncing round him like a spirited lamb and dogging his footprints with every sign of affection. Eventually, Mentor discovered that this touching display of affection was brought on by a large thorn in the animal's foot which it wanted him to remove.

Lions in those days seemed to be remarkably careless, for Pliny records another story by one Elpis which stretched even my credulity to the breaking point. Elpis had hardly set foot in Africa when he was accosted by a lion with open jaws. Not unnaturally, he fled to the nearest tree (calling upon Bacchus to preserve him) and stayed ensconced in the upper branches for some considerable time while the lion, still open-mouthed, wandered about below trying by various signs to show the dull-witted fellow what was wrong. Obviously, Elpis had not read much contemporary travel literature or he would have realized at once that the lion had a thorn or something it wanted him to remove. It was quite some time before it dawned on him that however fierce a lion might be it would not walk about with its mouth permanently open in that curious fashion. So he cautiously descended from the tree and found that the lion, true to form, had a bone wedged in its mouth. Elpis removed this at once and without, apparently, much difficulty. The lion was so overcome with joy and gratitude that it immediately appointed itself chief butcher to its rescuer's ship, and for the whole time that they were anchored in that region it provided the ship's company with fresh venison daily.

From these stories in Pliny and Purchas one gets the impression that in those days you could not go anywhere in Africa without being accosted by groups of mournful lions suffering from wounds, bones or thorns, which they expected you to cure for them.

Albert and his wives, unlike their ancestors, seemed to be remarkably healthy, and, to my relief, they never got thorns in their paws which they expected us to remove. They had prodigious appetites, in spite of being so fat, and would squabble and snarl over their meat as though they had not been fed for weeks. Albert would snatch the biggest joint and carry it off into the bushes and hide it. Then he would hastily return to see if he could pinch the joints belonging to either of his wives. To watch him cuff his wife out of the way while he stole her meat was a startling example of the lion's noble character.

Once a week we had to trap up Albert and his wives so that we could enter the cage and clean up the bones and other signs of their tenancy. Built into the side of the enclosure was a large, iron-barred trap with a sliding door, and we had to get all three lions securely locked up in this before we could get on with the work. This trapping up was a tedious performance, the monotony of which was relieved only by its ridiculousness. To trap Albert and his wives, who were, needless to say, uncooperative in the extreme, you had to be very cunning and combine this with the ability to look innocent and run fast. The first requisite for successful trapping was that Albert should be very hungry; he would then prowl along the bars, his little eyes glinting, his mane shaggy with ferocity. We would arrive at the trap, looking radiantly innocent, and place our various spades, buckets, brushes and forks on the path. Then we would produce a large, gory joint of meat and place it in a position where Albert could both see and smell it. He would greet this maneuver with a series of wicked, chuckling snarls deep in the scarf of his mane. Then we would raise the sliding door at the end of the trap and stand about, all talking loudly, as if there were no thought farther from our minds than the trapping of lions. I must explain, in defense of Albert's intelligence, that he was not fooled by all this for one minute, but it had become a sort of custom or ritual which had to be respected or the whole procedure would become disorganized.

When sufficient time had passed and Albert had studied the joint and pondered its possibilities, we would put it inside the trap. Leaning on the barrier rail, we would indulge in auto-suggestion. The following remarks would be made with complete lack of tone and interest: "How about it, Alb? Hungry, boy? Come on, then, come on. There's a good lad. Have some meat, then. Come on, then. Come on. Come on. . . ." We would repeat this endlessly, like a part song, and the whole performance was made doubly ridiculous by the fact that Albert understood none of it.

Having exhausted our encouraging remarks, we would reach a deadlock; we would glare at Albert and he would glare back at us. All through this Nan and Jill would be prowling in the background, obviously impatient but doing nothing, for tradition demanded that their lord and master should take the lead. Albert would now give the impression of having gone into a trance. During these spells of waiting I would while away the time by attempting to find an answer to that much disputed question of whether or not the human eye has any power over the mere beast. I would stare with intense concentration into Albert's little yellow eyes, and he would stare back unblinkingly. The only effect it ever had was to make me feel a trifle uncomfortable.

Generally, after about ten minutes Albert would still show no signs of entering the trap, and so we would be forced to try another ruse. Leaving the meat in the trap, we would saunter off down the path until Albert thought we were too far away to be dangerous. Then he would made a sudden dash into the trap, grab the meat, and endeavor to escape with it before we had time to rush down the path and slam the door on him. More often than not, the iron door clanged down some two inches behind his retreating tail and we would be left standing there foolishly while he carried his trophy off to some secluded spot to settle down and enjoy it. This, of course, would put an end to our trapping and we would be forced to wait twenty-four hours until Albert felt peckish again. With the other animals on the section we had to go through much the same business to get them trapped up, but they never gave us as much trouble as the lions. Albert had a genius for being annoying.

If, however, we did get the lions safely locked up in the trap, we had to make our way round to a small door in the opposite side of the cage. Once we had entered the enclosure we had to shut and lock this door behind us. It was a feeling I never really relished, for it meant that we were shut in a two-acre cage, surrounded by a barred fence some sixteen feet high, with no mean of escape should the lions, by some magical means, get out of the trap. On one occasion Joe and I entered the cage and, as usual, separated and worked our way through the bushes, picking up the gnawed white bones from last week's meals. Soon we lost sight of each other in the thick undergrowth; I could hear Joe whistling and an occasional clang as he dropped a bone into his bucket. I was working my way along a narrow path between great bramble bushes which must have been a favorite haunt of Albert's, for I could see his great paw marks in the soft clay of the path and, here and there, a tuft of hair from his mane which had caught on a thorn. I was musing over the big paw marks and thinking what a vicious and sultry character Albert was, when suddenly he roared. Now, the traps were some distance away through the trees, on my left, yet I could have sworn that the roar came from directly in front of me. Without waiting to find out exactly where Albert was, I made my way with all speed to the exit gate. Joe and I arrived at the gate simultaneously.

"Is he out?" I inquired when we were safely outside the cage.

"I don't know," said Joe. "I didn't wait to see."

We went round to the other side of the enclosure and found the lions still locked up in the trap, but Albert had a humorous glint in his eyes that made me think.

This incident was my first experience of the so-called ventriloquial powers of the lion. Many writers assert that a lion can throw his roar, so to speak, so that it appears to come from two or three different directions at once. This is not quite as impossible as it sounds, for many species of birds and insects have the most astonishing ventriloquial powers. In some cases you can actually watch the creature making the sound and yet the sound itself appears to come from several feet, or even yards, away. Obviously, if the lion possessed this power it would be immensely useful to him; he would be able to panic herds of game at night so that, in their terror, they might run toward their hunter instead of away from him. Judging by that morning's experience it certainly seemed as though Albert could throw his roar; he had been about the same distance away from Joe as from me, yet both of us were sure that the roar had come from close by.

46

Some time after this experience I had another and equally startling example of Albert's voice throwing. I was coming back from some village festivities late one night and I decided to take a shortcut through the park. My path took me along the side of the lion cage, and as I hurried along through the rustling elders Albert gave a sudden snarling grunt that brought me to a standstill. The sound was difficult to place, although I knew the direction from which it must have come. It had a certain earth-trembling quality that made it seem as though it was vibrating up through the soles of my feet. To judge by the sound, Albert might have been inside or outside his cage. It was not very pleasant, and only my devotion to natural history prevented me from running like a hare. With considerable temerity, I walked up to the barrier rail and peered into the gloom, but I could not see anything and there was no moon to help me. The bushes were black and still. As I moved along the side of the cage I knew that I was being followed; I could almost feel the eager eyes fixed on me, but the tawny bodies made no sound and the great paws did not snap a single twig as a guide to their whereabouts. As I started up the hillside, away from the cage, there came a great sniff, full of scorn and derision.

Some people refuse to believe that a lion can throw his voice deliberately. They maintain that all he does is hold his mouth close to the ground when roaring, so that the sound is blurred and it is impossible to tell from which direction it is coming. Now, in order to find out if this was true I tried very hard to be present when Albert was roaring, but with little success. Time after time I would walk hopefully past his cage thinking that he might roar while I was there to see, but every time he remained stubbornly silent. Sometimes, when I heard him start up, I would treat the visitors to the sight of a keeper running madly along the path through the trees as though some escaped beast were at my heels. But every time, when I arrived panting at the barrier rail, I would find that Albert had either finished or else had thought better of it and had relapsed into silence after two or three coughs. However, I was more than compensated for this by the magnificent sounds he would produce when I could hear but not see him.

He always seemed to choose the late afternoon to burst into song. He would start, quite suddenly, with two or three preliminary "Aroom" noises, with long pauses in between, as if he were making sure of the right note. Then he would launch into the full song: the "Arooms" would become throaty and rich and the pause between them shorter and shorter, until they ran together in a terrific crescendo of sound. It would rasp out, faster and faster, and then start to slow down; then, just as suddenly as it began, it would stop. It is difficult to describe the frightening possibilities that were snarled at you when the sound reached its zenith. Considered dispassionately, the song resembled, more than anything else, someone sawing wood on a gigantic echoing barrel. First there would be the slow strokes of the saw; then they would get faster and faster as the steel bit into the wood; then the strokes would get slow again, as an indication that the sawing was nearly done; then silence. And at that moment I always waited to hear the thud of the piece of wood hitting the ground.

After some weeks' association with Albert I decided that he did not in any way measure up to the popular estimation of what a lion should be. He was sulky, blustery and devoid of any finer feelings whatsoever. His small golden eyes always had in them an expression of baffled rage, as though he were trying to uphold his race's reputation for fierceness without knowing why. There was always a faintly puzzled look about him, as though he were wondering whether it was necessary to behave in this way. When he was not prowling about in a filthy temper he was indulging in his "joke" of jumping out suddenly at unsuspecting passersby and getting a sardonic pleasure out of their panic. At mealtimes he would behave in the most reprehensible manner I have described and then, gorged with his own meat and his ill-gotten gains, he would sprawl in the long grass and belch. I tried very hard, but I could not find a single endearing quality in Albert.

Only once during our association did I see him look really regal, and that was when Jill came into season. With his mane standing out, Albert strode about the cage uttering heart-rending "Urrghs" to himself and striking attitudes expressive of nobility and firmness of character. Pliny, I am sure, would have loved him. While Albert was following Jill round the cage I delved once more into Pliny to see what he had to say about the love life of the lion. The first reference I found was not very flattering:

> . . . these Lionesses are very letcherous, and this is the cause that the Lions are so fell and cruell. This, Affricke knoweth best, and seeth most: and especially in time of great drought, when for want of water a number of wild beasts resort by troups to those few rivers that be there, and meet together. And Hereupon it is, that so many strange shaped beasts, of a mixt and mungrell kind are there bred, whiles the males either perforce, or for pleasure, leape and cover the females of all sorts.

I never saw Nan and Jill behaving in a lecherous manner normally, and when in season they seemed more bored than anything else by Albert's attention. Pliny goes on to say:

> The Lion knoweth by sent and smell of the Pard, when the Lionesse his mate hath plaied false, and suffered herselfe to be covered by him: and presently with all his might and maine runneth upon her for to chastise and punish her.

This, of course, may be true. Certainly Nan and Jill had no chance of playing Albert false, since they were locked in the cage with him. But I do feel that Albert would have been a strict husband, and I should hate to have been his wife if I had been flirting with a Pard and he had caught me.

Why visitors looked furtively at each other and giggled when Albert performed an act of procreation, with great dignity and complete lack of embarrassment, in the middle of a clearing was always a source of bewilderment to me. They would have been doubly disgusted if they had known that it was his daughter, Jill, who was participating in the orgy. Incest!

Joe was also afflicted with this curious shyness when he came across an example of coition and would, in fact, carefully avoid any cages in which he knew such dreadful acts were taking place. Jesse, on the other hand, possessed no such reticence. In a hoarse voice he would shout libelous encouragements to the animals while the crowd shuffled and dispersed around him. Jesse was a past master at the art of making a crowd disappear like a puff of smoke.

"How he can *do* it, I don't know," Joe would confide in me when we were safely in the sexless harbor of The Haven. "I go hot and cold all over, honest I do. Only yesterday I went along by the lions and there he was talking to 'em all, young girls and everything, and old Albert was there with Jill, plain as hell. I don't know how he does it. I couldn't, not for a hundred pounds."

He would purse his lips and look very sad, as though he were really refusing the money. Poor Joe, his life was not worth living when any of the animals were in season.

Apart from his cavalier attitude toward the facts of life, Jesse was possessed of a curious power that won the grudging envy of both Joe and myself. As a dowser can feel water in the bones of his hand and make a hazel twig twitch over a hidden spring, as a truffle hound can scent the delicious fungus though it lurks ever so deeply belowground, so Jesse was capable, by some strange wizardry, of spotting a tip. He would stand just outside The Haven, sucking his teeth and surveying the passing throng of visitors; suddenly he would stiffen, his frost-white eyebrows would quiver, he would crack his teeth together with a small sort of satisfied snap. "There's two bob," he would say and commence to stalk his prey with all the cunning of one of the great cats in his charge. Try as we would, Joe and I could never see any difference between the people that Jesse got into conversation with and the people that we got into conversation with, but Jesse had an unerring instinct and could estimate before his attack the precise amount of money that he was going to extract from the person concerned. He would have made a splendid pirate.

"Don't know how he does it, the old bugger," said Joe to me. "Look, the other day he says to me, 'You try your luck, Joe. There's a good 'un just going up by the polars—that chap in the trilby. He's good for five bob.' Well, I went up and spent half an hour with the bloke, told him all sorts of things. I was as nice as pie with him, honest, and all I got out of him was a bleeding Woodbine cigarette."

I am afraid that after a time I got rather bored with Albert and his females. They lacked the personality that the other animals on the section possessed. Also, they refused to be friendly in any way whatsoever and so you could not really get to know them. I found Pliny's imaginary lions and lion stories much more interesting than the live specimens we looked after. I do not know if Albert realized that I had little affection for him, but he suddenly seemed to take an intense dislike to me and made noisy and alarming attempts to slaughter me whenever I went near the cage. He nearly succeeded, too.

One day Joe decided that we would clean out the drains alongside the lion cage so that I would have something to remember when I moved to another section. We went along there, armed with a hose, forks, brushes and other implements, and after a time managed to get Albert and Co. into the traps. Then, while Joe wielded the hose, whistling merrily, I climbed inside the barrier rail and worked my way along, cleaning all the accumulated debris out of the drain. I had to get close to accomplish this, and that was the reason that Albert had to be trapped up, for the bars in the cage were quite wide enough for him to get his paw through but those on the trap were closer together. We were getting along fine, when I came to the bit of drain that ran alongside the traps where Albert was simmering with rage. Joe had been squirting the hose about with gay abandon and everything was dripping with water. As I stood up to reach for a broom my foot slipped and I fell against the side of the trap. It was fortunate that

52

the bars on it were no wider or Albert would have had me by the shoulder. As it was, he lost no time in springing at me with a triumphant snarl and trying to get his paw between the bars to dig his claws into me. He managed to get only a small part of his toes through but he got one claw firmly hooked in the sleeve of my coat. Joe, uttering a yelp of alarm and obviously under the impression that I was being mauled, turned the hose in our direction. He meant, of course, to squirt the water in Albert's face and make him release me. However, in his excitement he misjudged, and just as I had torn myself free of Albert's claw and was leaping away, I received the full jet of the hose in my face and was sent reeling and spluttering back against the trap. Albert had another attempt at hooking me and failed; Joe squirted the hose again and it hit me between the eyes. I got away from the traps and climbed over the barrier rail, dripping water,

"Whose side are you supposed to be on?" I asked Joe.

"Sorry," he said contritely, "but I thought the old swine had got you."

"You certainly gave him every opportunity to do so," I said bitterly, mopping myself with an inadequate handkerchief.

Twice a week it was my duty during the long summer evenings to stay on the section after Jesse and Joe had left, to make sure that no members of the public displayed their intelligence by climbing a barrier rail or throwing bottles at the animals. I found these evenings very pleasant. I was lord of all I surveyed; I would sit in The Haven over a strong cup of tea, trying to make sense of my hurried notes and get them into some sort of order. Gradually, outside, the shadows would lengthen across the turf and the last little clusters of people would move toward the main gate. It was very quiet when the crowds had gone, and the wallabies would hop cautiously from the shelter of the elder bushes where they had been driven during the day by shouting hordes of little boys. Albert would give a few husky "Arooms" to get his voice in trim for the night's concert, and you would hear quite clearly the splash and splish of the polar bears lounging in their pool.

My last duty before leaving was to walk the length of the section to see that everything was all right. The wallabies would be scattered over the turf, feeding quietly, soothed by the sudden hush that followed the retreating visitors. The tigress Ranee would be glad to have the door of her den opened, for the great cement pit in which she lived was now in shadow and cold to the paws. Paul, her son, would be already asleep in his bed of straw. Farther along, across the Downs, the raccoonlike dogs would be curled up tightly in their little wooden hutches, while next to them the arctic foxes flitted like pale shadows among the bushes. Ahead of me, down the path, the wallabies would scatter in fright, bouncing and crashing through the undergrowth. The lions would be lying in the long grass by the edge of their pool; Albert, sunk in his mane, meditating as usual, while beside him Nan and Jill would sleep, with bulging stomachs. There would be wallabies everywhere rocking slowly across the turf, dragging their heavy tails behind them. Flocks of magpies would flap and chuck in the treetops. In the tiger dell Jum and his mate would be drowsing, while around their cage the bushes would crack and rustle with wallabies. Wallabies, wallabies, wallabies everywhere; and in the gloom of the elder spinneys you could hear their rabbitlike teeth rasping the bark from the trees.

Having assured myself that all was right with the section, and spurred on by the thought of the especially enormous tea that Mrs. Bailey always gave me when I was on late night duty, I would take my leave. On the way out there was always the empty bottle to pick up or the scrap of sandwich paper.

CHAPTER 3

A Triumph of Tigers

———————◆———————

*Will find a Tiger will repay the trouble
and expense.*
—BELLOC, *The Tiger*

ON our arrival in the morning the sunshine would be barely warm, but it would give a brittle gold burnish to the leaves and grass, and in its clear light you could see and hear the park becoming awake. Among the lurching shapes of the elders, with trails of mist still entangled in their branches, droves of wallabies would squat in this quiet morning sun, plump bodies flaccid, their fur furrowed with dew. Clearly, echoing across the paddocks, would come the strident "Help . . . *help!*" of a peacock, dragging its colored tail through the pine woods. The zebras, as you passed, would throw up their heads and snort great fountains of steam at you and take nervous, prancing steps in the wet grass. Turn onto the gravel path that led to the section, and the polar bears would point quivering black noses at you from between the bars of their cage, sniffing in anguished anticipation at the rich smell of the loaves under your arm. Jesse and Joe would walk on to the hut while I went down into the tiger pit. The iron gate would clatter, shaking a thousand vibrating echoes from the walls of the cement dungeons, and I would go inside to do the first jobs of the day.

The tigers would wake and greet me with pink-mouthed, misty yawns, lying there luxuriously in their beds of yellow rustling straw. Then they would stretch elegantly—long, curved-backed, stiff-tailed, nose-quivering stretches—before padding across their dens to peer at me through the barred doors. In this pit lived two of our four tigers, Paul and Ranee, who were mother and son. But Paul cherished no affection for his parent, so they had to sleep in separate dens and they were let out into the pit in turn. My first job in the morning was to let Ranee out of her den into the pit; I would pull back the heavy sliding door and close it again when she had slouched out into the sunlight. Then I would spend an illegal five minutes feeding her son on strips of meat.

Paul was the largest and the finest of the tigers. He had such a languid perfection of movement and such a placid temperament that it was hard to believe that Ranee was really his mother. He moved silently and unhurriedly on his great pincushion paws; his mother moved just as silently but in a quick, nervous, jerky sort of way that was unpleasantly suggestive of her ability to catch you unawares. I am quite sure that she spent most of her spare time trying to evolve a successful method of killing us. She had a savage streak in her which showed in her unblinking green eyes. Paul would take meat from my hand with an air of quiet dignity and great gentleness; his mother would gulp at it ferociously and, if given the chance, take your hand as well. With Paul you got the impression that your hand, even if offered, would be considered an inferior object and, as such, ignored. It was a comforting thought, even if incorrect.

During these morning talks I had with him, Paul was so avuncular that it was only with difficulty that I remembered he *could* be dangerous if he wanted to be; he would curve his huge head against the bars and let me scratch his ears, purring loudly, so that he seemed more like a giant domestic cat than the popular conception of a bloodthirsty tiger. He would accept my gifts of meat with a regal condescension and, having eaten them, would lie down and lick his paws while I would squat enraptured and gaze at him. At such close quarters he was fascinating to watch. Every inch of his richly colored body was beautifully proportioned, and its movements were liquid and graceful. His head was massive, very broad between the ears, and the ruff round his chin was evenly curved and of the palest saffron color. Across his bright

hide the stripes sprawled like black flames. Perhaps the most beautiful part of him was his eyes: large and almond-shaped, set slanting in his face, like sea-polished pebbles of leaf green.

Usually my morning talk with Paul was cut short by Jesse, who would want to know where the so-and-so I had got to with his spade. Fetching this spade was the excuse I used every morning to spend a little time with the tigers. This implement was an essential part of Jesse's routine; with it he would disappear among the trees for his early-morning catharsis, without which a day's work would be unthinkable.

When Jesse had returned from his communion with nature we would set to work and clean the tiger pit. First, Ranee would be locked up in her den again while we went into the pit with brushes and buckets and scrubbed the concrete down and collected the bones from yesterday's dinner. Then Ranee and Paul would be let out, in turn, so that we could clean their dens and give them fresh beds. When we let them back into their dens they would perform a most curious action. They would walk straight to their straw beds, sniffing about them, and then they would stand in the center of the bed and proceed to knead and pad the straw with their paws. Their ears would be laid back and their eyes, half closed, would be dreamy and thoughtful. Then, rising suddenly, they would urinate copiously and accurately into the middle of their clean beds. This done, they would relax and spend the rest of the morning dozing, sometimes licking their paws and then yawning ponderously. I think that when they entered their dens and found fresh straw beds, clean sawdust on the floor, and their own strong odor temporarily downed by the smell of the disinfectant we splashed on the walls and floor, they wished to prove to themselves (and any chance visitors) that the dens were part of their territory. To do this they injected the straw with their own pungent smell again. Then, having, as it were, hoisted the flag, they could settle down and await feeding time.

When we had cleaned the pit, the three of us would retire to The Haven for a light snack. In the gloomy interior we would perch on our creaking chairs and examine each other's food packets with interest. Jesse, his sandwich held in a large red hand, would eat slowly and methodically, but with complete lack of interest. Joe would gallop through his food, talking jovially to me with his mouth full, punctuating his remarks with bursts of his curious husky laughter. He is the only person I have ever met whose laugh could be accurately written as "he he he." Jesse would remain gloomily silent; when he had finished his food he would gaze vacantly out the window, sucking his teeth. Then with reptilian slowness, he would light his pipe and suck and squeak and bubble over it while Joe and I discussed the weather, fishing, the best way to skin a rabbit, or the comparative merits of the three blondes whose portraits adorned the wall above Joe's chair. Presently we would rise and make our way out of the hut to finish the next job on the list, the cleaning of the polar-bear cage. Outside The Haven, in the tangled web of elder branches, magpies would chuck suspiciously as we appeared and Joe would give a tremendous, boisterous shout that would burst them from among the leaves like chattering piebald arrows.

The meat would be delivered early in the day—great bloodstained haunches covered with green splotches of dye to denote that they were unfit for human consumption. Then from two-thirty to three we would be busy hacking those joints down to size, stacking them in buckets and deciding which particular animals should have any tidbits like heart or liver. Then at three o'clock the feeding would commence.

We always started with the Tiger Dell (known to us as the bottom tigers), which was the furthermost point of the section. Here, in a great cage like the lions', filled with tangled undergrowth, lived Jum and Maurena, who were in no way related to Paul and Ranee in the pit. Two of us would set out bearing buckets containing the meat. Invariably we would be followed by a crowd of small urchins and a sprinkling of adults who had appeared, apparently, from nowhere. The children would scutter round us, uttering shrill exclamations, asking questions, pushing and jumping in their eagerness to view the gory joints from the best positions.

"Cor! Look at the meat. Alf! *Alf!* Look at the meat!"

"Wot's the fork for, mister?"

"Coo! Bet they won't half *eat* that."

"Wot kind of meat is it, mister?"

"Mind, John dear, don't get in the keeper's way. John, do you hear?"

And so on, until we reached the tiger cage, where Jum and Maurena would be slithering up and down the bars in frantic eagerness.

Feeding these two tigers was always more interesting, from my point of view, than feeding Paul and his mother, for in the pit the meat was simply flung over the side to them, but with the bottom tigers the proceedings were more intimate. We would stab a joint of meat on the fork, and the thin end, usually the knuckle bone, would be inserted through the bars. Jum, with a perfect display of gentlemanly instincts, would snarl and cuff at his mate should she try to bite on this. Grasping the end of the joint in his mouth, he would brace his feet against the stonework, and with arched back and swelling muscles he would start to pull. It was incredible and rather frightening, this display of strength, for the joint was dragged through the bars inch by inch, the bars *bending* to allow it entrance. It would come free suddenly, throwing him back on his haunches; then, with the joint in his mouth and his head held high, he would swagger off through the bushes to eat it down by the pond.

Jum and Maurena fed, we would retrace our steps to the pit in order to replenish our buckets. Again we would be followed by a knot of onlookers and have to face the barrage of silly questions that tiger feeding always seemed to bring on.

"Why is the meat raw?"

"Would they eat it if you cooked it?"

"Why has a tiger got stripes?"

"Would they bite you if you went in with them?"

This sort of question was generally asked by adults; the children asked much more sensible questions, as a rule.

Although Paul was my favorite among the tigers, Jum and Maurena were, I had to admit, the best show. Moving against a green background of bushes and trees, their color seemed more vivid than ever. They were a bad-tempered pair, however, and I never ceased to marvel at the speed of mind and body that could change them from indolent, swaying animals to hissing, snarling personifications of anger. Another thing that endeared Jum and his mate to me was the curious little chats they would have with each other, employing a most unusual method of conversation. This was so far removed from the range of sounds they produced when growling or snarling that it could be classified as a separate language. It consisted entirely of sniffs, and prodigious, bubbling, nose-quivering sniffs they were, too. It was quite incredible, the variation they could achieve and the different meaning they could impart (or that I imagined they could impart) by means of this simple noise. The only time they conversed in this way was when we were trapping them up or when they had just been released from the traps. They had two distinct ways of producing this sniffing, and each was capable of variation according to circumstances. With the first method, the noise was prolonged and sonorous, like a quietly muttered conversation; in the second method the sniffs were startlingly loud and interrogative. Both the tigers took part in these chats, and when one delivered itself of a questioning sniff the other would always give some sort of an answer. At first I could distinguish only the two main themes, as it were: the mutter and the question. By listening carefully, however, I could hear that each of these themes seemed to vary very slightly as it was delivered, so that each sniff seemed to have its own meaning and each seemed different from the other. At first when I heard one of these conversations I merely thought that the tigers were sniffing; then it seemed to me that they were really talking to each other in a very primitive form of language. I was so intrigued by this idea that I spent a lot of time mastering a few of the more simple sniff sounds, and then I went back to the pit and practiced on Paul. When he came to his door to talk to me I filled my lungs with air and gave forth a rich, prolonged questioning sniff that I was sure could not have been done better by Jum himself. I was hoping that Paul would answer me. He stopped, obviously startled, and retreated a few steps. I gave another sniff, almost as good as the first, and with less waste of spittle; I felt I was getting into my

stride. I looked at Paul hopefully. He directed on me a look
so full of scorn that I almost blushed; then he turned his back
on me and slouched off back to his bed. I felt that I should
have practiced a bit more before trying it on him.

It was during the time that I was trying to master this tiger
language that I first met Billy. I had been down to look at the
lions and on the way back I was practicing my tiger sniffs.
I rounded a corner, giving vent to a really full-blooded sniff
and almost ran into a tall, lanky youth with a mop of red hair,
circular blue eyes, a snub nose, his upper lip and chin covered
with a fine egg-yolk-yellow down.

"Hello," he said, grinning at me ingratiatingly, "you're the
new bloke."

"Yes," I said. "Who are you?"

He waved his arms about like windmills and giggled.

"I'm Billy," he said; "just call me Billy. Everybody calls
me Billy."

"What section do you work on?" I inquired, as I had not
seen him before.

"Oh, all over," said Billy, glancing at me sideways, slyly,
"all over."

We stood in silence for a moment while Billy stared at me
with the avid interest of a naturalist who has come across a
new species.

"That's a very bad cold you've got," he said suddenly.

"I haven't got a cold," I said, surprised.

"You have," said Billy accusingly. "I could hear you sneezing all down the path."

"I wasn't sneezing," I said; "I was sniffing."

"Well, it sounded like sneezing," said Billy aggrievedly.

"Well, it wasn't," I said firmly. "It was sniffing. I was practicing my tiger sniffs."

Billy stared at me, round-eyed.

"Practicing your what?" he asked.

"Tiger sniffs," I said. "The tigers talk to each other in sniffs and I'm trying to learn how to do it."

"You must be balmy," said Billy with conviction. "How can you talk in sniffs?"

"Well, the tigers do," I said. "You should listen to them sometime."

Billy giggled. "Do you like working here?" he inquired.

"Yes," I said, "very much. Don't you?"

He glanced at me slyly again.

"Yes, but it's different for me; I have to be here," he said.

I decided at this point that as every village was reputed to have an idiot, I had stumbled across the one belonging to Whipsnade.

"Well, I must be getting along," I said.

"I'll see you later," said Billy.

"Yes, I expect so," I said.

As he loped off through the elder bushes he suddenly burst into song in a shrill, ear-splitting voice.

> *"A wandering minstrel I,*
> *A thing of rags and tatters . . ."*

I made my way back to The Haven, where I found Joe manufacturing a trout fly for himself.

"I've just met the village idiot," I said.

"Village idiot?" said Joe. "What's that, then?"

"I don't know," I said. "A tall redheaded boy called Billy."

"Idiot?" said Joe. "He's no idiot. Don't you know who he is?"

"No," I said curiously, "who is he?"

"He's Captain Beale's son," said Joe.

"Good Lord!" I said. "I wish you'd warned me."

I hastily ran over in my mind my conversation with Billy, trying to remember whether I had said anything particularly insulting.

"Well, where does he work?" I asked. "Which section?"

"He doesn't," said Joe. "He just drifts around—gives a hand here and there. More trouble than he's worth sometimes, but he's a nice boy."

My meeting with Billy soon faded from my mind, for I had other, more important things to occupy me. Maurena, the tigress, had come into season and now I had the pleasure of watching the tigers' courtship. Luckily, it happened on my official day off, so I spent the whole day down at the bottom tigers' concealed in a strategic spot, making copious notes.

From early morning Jum had been following his mate around like a tawny shadow, belly-crawling, abject, heavy with passion. From where I stood among the trees I could see them in the checkered shadows of the bushes, the sun glinting on their flanks as they moved. Jum walked behind and a little to one side of his mate. He kept his distance, for early in the day he had approached too close and she had resented it. His muzzle bore three deep red grooves as proof of her reticence. She seemed to have changed overnight from the timid, servile creature she was normally, to a slinking, dangerous animal that dealt with his premature advances speedily and fero-

ciously. Jum seemed to be puzzled by this metamorphosis; to have their positions reversed so suddenly and completely must have been a considerable surprise to him.

They paced up and down among the elder trunks, and presently Jum's love overwhelmed him again and he moved closer to Maurena, giving a purring moan in his throat, his eyes frosty with desire. Maurena did not cease her leisured pacing at his approach but merely lifted her lip over pink gums and chalk-white teeth. The moan died quickly in Jum's throat and he returned to his former position. They continued to pace back and forth, their tawny coats glowing in the shadowy twilight of the bushes. It seemed to me, waiting

uncomfortably among the nettles, that she would never yield, and I marveled at Jum's patience. Maurena seemed to relish this mastery over her mate, for another half hour's pacing was indulged in and Jum's movements were getting more and more jerkily impatient with every minute.

Then, as I watched, Maurena's walk become slower and more flaccid, her back curved until her pale honey-colored belly almost brushed the ground. She swayed more from side to side, and the expression in her eyes changed from one of weary preoccupation to the dreamy, mysterious expression that tigers assume when they drowse and muse after their food. Languidly, seeming more to drift, she came down from the tangle of trees, down to where the grass was long and thick by the pond. Here she paused and pondered with drooping head. Jum watched her eagerly from the edge of the trees, his eyes like frozen green leaves in the fierceness of his face. Maurena started to purr gently, the tip of her tail twitching among the grasses like a great black bumblebee. She yawned delicately, showing the pink inside of her mouth and the scalloped black edge to her lips. Slowly her body relaxed, and she toppled over and lay on her side in the grass. Jum moved swiftly toward her, rumbling interrogatively, and she answered with a blurred vibration in her throat. Quickly he was astride her, back arched, paws paddling along her ribs; as she raised her head, he bit with savage tenderness along the line of her arched neck. She seemed to melt under him, to become softer, until she was almost hidden in the grass. Presently they lay close together, asleep in the sun.

A thing that Jum used to do which I never saw the other tigers imitate was to lick his meat. The rasplike qualities of a tiger's tongue have to be seen to be believed. Once we fed Jum when he was confined in the trap, and so I could watch him eating within a foot or so of me. First, he nibbled off all the tatters and shreds of meat on the joint. Then he held it between his paws and started to lick the smooth red surface of the meat. As his long tongue curved over the flesh it made a sound like sandpaper drawn slowly over wood. The meat was literally shredded off by the abrasive qualities of his tongue, and where the flesh had been smooth it became rough and stood up in little points and tufts, like the pile on a carpet. He continued this for about ten minutes, and at the end of this time he had *licked* off about half an inch of meat. With such a formidable tongue, tigers need hardly use their teeth when feeding.

The only drawback to trying to observe the actions and habits of Jum and Maurena was that they had a very large and thickly overgrown area in which to live, and this made any consistent watching difficult. However, they were perhaps the best of tigers to watch, for they lived a very natural life. With Paul and Ranee you could never be sure if some habit was natural or something that they had invented because it fitted in with their unnatural life in the great concrete pit. Bathing was one of these things. I never saw Jum or Maurena enter their pool, nor, for that matter, did Paul ever do so. But Ranee, during the spells of hot weather, would take herself down to the pool and submerge her striped body in the cool water, leaving only her head and the tip of her tail out. She would sprawl there for sometimes half an hour, looking very coy and daring and occasionally twitching the tip of her tail to send the water splashing over her head. This most untiger-like action would provoke much comment and speculation among the members of the public who observed it.

"Agnes, come and look at this tiger in the water."

"Oh! Isn't it sweet?"

"Wonder why she does it."

"Dunno. Maybe she's thirsty."

"Well, what she want to lie in it for?"

"Dunno. Maybe she's ill."

"Don't be silly, Bert."

"Maybe she's a water tiger. Kind of special type, ay?"

"Yes, I suppose that's it. Isn't she *sweet*?"

"Throw her a bit of bread, Bert."

A large crust of bread would hit Ranee on the head and she would look up with a growl.

"No, she won't eat it."

"Try a peanut."

Now, it may be difficult to believe, but the above conversation is not a figment of my imagination. I wrote it down as it was spoken, and I have someone who was witness to it. The sight of Ranee lolling in the water produced the weirdest theories on the part of the great British public. They would cluster round the rail and stare down at her with intense concentration. They could not have displayed more interest if it had been a street accident.

Before going to work at Whipsnade I never realized how ignorant people are about even the commonest facts of animal life. The keepers, however, were supposed to know the answers to everything. Were tigers born with stripes? Would the lions bite you if you went in with them? Why had a tiger stripes and a lion none? Why had a lion a mane and a tiger none? Would the tigers bite you if you went in with them? Why were polar bears white? Where did they come from? Would *they* bite if you went in with them? These questions, and hundreds of others, were asked every day of the week, sometimes twenty or thirty times a day. On a crowded day the wear and tear on one's temper was quite considerable.

Many visitors I chatted to were surprised and rather disappointed to find that we did not spend our days cheating death by inches at the claws of a lion or a bear. I had no livid scars to show for my work, and this seemed to make me, in their eyes, something of a charlatan. You got the impression that it was an insult to ask them to believe that life among such animals was, on the whole, a very peaceful affair. According to them, my clothes should have been in tatters, my head bloody but unbowed, and my day one long series of hair-raising experiences. On looking back, it seems to me that I lost an excellent opportunity of making money. If I had slashed my coat to ribbons, rubbed myself all over with a few gory joints, and then staggered out of the pit every half hour or so remarking nonchalantly, "That tiger's the devil to groom!" I might have been rich by now.

Visitors, on the whole, caused us a lot of trouble and, sometimes, a lot of amusement. Two things I shall always remember. The first was a small boy who, after watching me feeding the tigers, approached me, wide-eyed, and asked in a hushed voice, "Mister, 'ave you ever been ate by one of them buggers?" The other incident was when a small boy, his face red with excitement, came dashing down the path toward the pit. He looked over the side hastily, saw Paul pacing up and down, and turned to shout to his family. "Mum!" he yelled. "Mum, come here quick and look at this zebra."

It was some days after I had met Billy for the first time that I saw him again. He came down the path that led to the lions, bouncing and clanking his way on an ancient and rusty bicycle. I had just finished cutting a thick bed of nettles that were overgrowing the path and was pausing for a much needed cigarette.

"Hello," said Billy shrilly, clamping the brakes on his bicycle so hard that he almost shot over the handlebars. He straddled the bicycle with his long, gangly legs and grinned at me inanely.

"Hello," I said cautiously.

"What you doing?" he inquired.

"Cutting nettles," I said.

"I hate that job," said Billy. "I always get stung, sometimes in the most peculiar places."

"So do I," I said with feeling.

Billy glanced about him nervously. "I say," he said in a conspiratorial whisper, "you haven't got a cigarette on you, have you?"

"Sure," I said, and gave him one.

He lit it inexpertly and puffed at it vigorously.

"You won't tell anybody, will you?" he said. "I'm not supposed to smoke."

"Where are you off to?" I inquired.

Billy swallowed some smoke the wrong way and coughed violently for some time, his eyes streaming.

"Nothing like a good smoke," he said hoarsely.

"It doesn't seem to be doing you much good," I said.

"Oh, but I enjoy it very much."

"Well, where are you off to?" I asked again.

"I've come to see you," he said waving his cigarette at me. The end of it was now dangling, limp with spittle.

"Oh," I said, "what do you want to see me about?"

"Daddy wants you to come to drinks this evening," said Billy

I stared at him with astonishment. "*Your* father wants *me* to come to drinks?" I said in amazement. "Are you serious?"

Billy, having imbibed another lungful of smoke, was seized with another paroxysm of coughing and could only nod his head wildly, his red hair flapping up and down.

"Well, what does he want *me* to come to drinks for?" I asked, greatly puzzled.

"Thinks . . ." gasped Billy, "thinks you might be good influence on me."

"Dear God," I said, "I've no intention of being a good influence on anybody and, anyway, I could hardly be called a good influence when I've just given you a cigarette and you're not supposed to smoke."

"Don't tell anybody," croaked Billy. "Secret. See you at six-thirty."

Still gasping and choking, he clanked off into the undergrowth on his bicycle.

So at six that evening I put on my only pair of respectable trousers, a coat and a tie, and presented myself at the Beale establishment, which occupied one end of the administration block in the park. Although I had learned from other members of the staff that Captain Beale's gruff exterior hid a heart of gold, I was still slightly apprehensive, for, after all, he was the superintendent of the place and I was the lowest of the low.

The door was opened to me by Mrs. Beale, who was a charming, handsome woman with an air of unruffled calm.

"Do come in," she said, smiling at me sweetly. "May I call you Gerry? Billy keeps calling you Gerry. Come into the drawing room—the captain's there."

She ushered me into the large, pleasant living room, where in one corner, lying supine in an enormous chair, was the vast bulk of Captain Beale, almost completely obliterated by the *Evening News*. Faint rumblings as from an incipient Krakatoa emanated from beneath the newspaper and it crackled and rustled as it rose and fell with the captain's breathing.

"Oh, dear," said Mrs. Beale. "I'm so sorry, he's dropped off. William! William! Gerry Durrell's here."

There was a noise like several freight trains colliding, and the captain surged up from under the newspaper like a leviathan surfacing.

"Hrumph," he croaked, straightening his spectacles and glaring at me owlishly. "Durrell, eh? Durrell? Glad to meet you. I mean, glad to have you."

He got to his feet, shedding pages of newspaper like autumn leaves falling off an enormous oak.

"Gladys," he barked, "give the boy a drink. Don't keep him standing there!"

Mrs. Beale treated this curt order as though it had never been uttered.

"Do sit down," she said, smiling. "What would you like to drink?"

At that time, just after the war, spirits were still as precious as gold, and although I longed for something like a whisky and soda to give me courage to talk with the captain, I knew that it would be impolite to say so.

"I'll just have a beer, if I may," I said.

While Mrs. Beale was fetching my drink the captain rumbled over to the fire and prodded it vigorously, obviously in the hopes of coaxing it into some sort of action. Several large glowing pieces of log fell out into the hearth and what little flame there had been withered and died. The captain flung down the poker aggrievedly.

"Gladys!" he roared. "The fire's out!"

"Well, stop poking it, dear," said Mrs. Beale. "You know you always put it out."

The captain hurled himself into the chair, and the springs screeched protestingly.

"Bloody awful stuff, this wartime beer, don't you think,

Durrell?" he observed, eyeing the glass that Mrs. Beale was handing to me.

"Don't swear, dear," said Mrs. Beale.

"Bloody awful stuff," said the captain defiantly, glaring at me. "Don't you agree, Durrell?"

"Well, I didn't drink beer before the war, so I don't really know," I said.

"Not a hop in it," said the captain. "Mark my words, not a hop in it."

Just at that moment Billy loped into the room as disjointedly as a giraffe.

"Hello," he said, grinning at me inanely. "You've arrived, have you?"

"Where have you been?" barked the captain.

"Out with Molly," said Billy, waving his arms about, "tra la la, tra la la, she's my girl friend now."

"Ha!" said the captain with satisfaction. "Out with girls, eh? That's the spirit! You a ladies' man, Durrell?"

"Well, I think so," I said cautiously, not being sure what Captain Beale's definition of a ladies' man was.

Glancing round to make sure that Mrs. Beale had left the room, the captain leaned forward in his chair.

"Used to be a bit of a gay dog with the ladies myself," he rumbled in a conspiratorial whisper. "Before I met Gladys, of course. Gad! Once you'd done a tour on the West Coast you needed the company of a good woman!"

"Were you very long in Africa?" I asked.

"Twenty-five years—twenty-five years. The blacks loved me," he said, with a sort of innocent boastfulness. " 'Course, I always treated them fairly; they appreciated that. Uncle Billy, they used to call me."

Billy, for some reason best known to himself, went off into peals of hysterical giggles at this.

"Uncle Billy!" he sputtered. "Fancy calling you Uncle Billy!"

"What's wrong with that?" snarled the captain. "Sign of affection. They had respect for me, I can tell you."

"Can I have a beer?" asked Billy.

"Only one," snapped the captain. "You're too young to drink. Tell him he's too young to drink, Durrell. Too young for drinking, smoking and lechery."

Billy screwed up his face and winked at me and then disappeared from the room in search of his beer.

"How are you getting on with the zebras?" asked Captain Beale suddenly.

He barked it out with such vehemence that I almost dropped my beer.

"Um, well, I have *seen* them," I said. "As a matter of fact, I'm on the lions."

"Ah," said the captain, "that's where you got to, is it? Well, how are you getting on with the lions?"

"Very well, I think," I said cautiously.

"Good," said the captain, dismissing this as a topic of conversation. "Do you like curry?"

"Um, yes, I do," I said.

"*Hot* curry?" inquired Captain Beale, glaring at me suspiciously.

"Yes. My mother makes very hot curries," I said.

"Good," said the captain with satisfaction. "Come to dinner —Thursday. I'll make a curry. Never let Gladys do it, she never makes it hot enough—wishy-washy stuff. There's nothing like a good sweat."

"It's very kind of you, sir."

"Gladys!" roared Captain Beale with a stentorian bellow that made the walls shake. "Durrell's coming to dinner Thursday. I'll make a curry."

"Very well, dear," said Mrs. Beale, coming back into the room. "Come about seven, Gerry."

"It's very kind of you," I said again.

"Excellent," said the captain, getting to his feet, "Thursday, then, ay?"

It was obvious that I was bidden to go.

"Well, thank you very much for the drink, sir," I said.

"Pleasure," rumbled the captain, "pleasure. Watch out for those zebras, mind; they can be nasty devils, you know. Good night."

CHAPTER 4

A Plash
of Polars

But the she-bear thus accosted rends the
peasant tooth and nail.
    —KIPLING, *The Female of the Species*

THE polar bears, Babs and Sam, were really the star performers of the section as far as the public were concerned. "Once you've seen them polars," Jesse would say to a visitor, "you've seen everything worthwhile in the place." The public liked to shudder over the real or imaginary fierceness of the lions and tigers, but once having seen them they lost interest. The polars, however, they never tired of watching, for the bears made them laugh. With the lions and tigers you had to watch them carefully for lengthy periods to extract any item of interest from their private lives, and most of the visitors had not the time to watch sleeping animals for lengthy periods in the hopes that their patience would be rewarded by some display of primitive passions or some example of the Wonders of Nature. But the polar bears were different: they were always on show, and people would stand by the hour and watch them. Sam would stand in one corner of the cage, swaying gently, or else he would lie prostrate on the concrete in the way you sometimes see dogs lying, with the hind legs splayed out, eyeing the public with a considerable scorn. Babs, his wife, would dive and swim for bits of bread and biscuit in the pool or else stick her long nose through the bars and open her mouth wide to have these tidbits thrown into it.

The difference between Babs and Sam was very marked, even at a cursory glance. Sam was huge and shaggy, with a tremendous rolling behind; his mate was sleek and slim. Sam's head was very broad across the skull, with small neat ears and the extraordinary bulge of flesh across the muzzle, the Roman nose of the old male polar. This fleshy protuberance would have made him look cunning if it had not been for the small good-humored eyes deep-set in his fur. Babs's head was long and narrow, balanced like an icicle on the sinuous length of her neck. Her expression *was* cunning and the whites of her eyes were tinged with yellow, an unprepossessing color that gave her the look of a jaded old woman on the morning after a hectic party. Sam, being the elder of the two, took life very slowly and sedately, plodding heavily round the cage like a benign and absent-minded old man. He never took two steps where one would do and, for the most part, did nothing very much except sleep in the sun. To contrast this, Babs was never still; if she was not waltzing about aimlessly she was crouched up by the bars, hooking at bits of biscuit and interesting bits of paper left by her admirers, or else splashing in the green waters of the pool.

At feeding time Babs would come to the bars and open her long mouth full of curved yellow teeth so that Jesse could throw bits of meat into it. Sam would never do anything so undignified; he would take the meat carefully in his amazingly prehensile lips and then drop it on the cement for examination. If the meat was encrusted with fat he would place a large paw on it, and then with his front teeth he would delicately pull the rustling fat off and eat it with great clops of his jaws and much lip-smacking. At feeding time Babs would always give a wonderful swimming display, but she could never persuade Sam to join in. She liked nothing better than a good audience, whose shouts and laughter would incite her to even greater heights of artistry; Sam did not give a damn whether there were people round the cage or not.

Babs would always spend half her day in the pool, regardless of weather conditions, rollicking about and making the green waters slop and splash. Sometimes she would lie on her back in the water for minutes at a time, examining her paws with intense concentration. I could never discover the reason for this strange habit. Most of the time she would swim the length of the pool as a dog would, all four feet thrusting the water; when she reached the end she would turn on her back and, with a strong kick from her hind legs against the side, would push herself off again, a crumple of foam about her neck and shoulders. Sam, as I say, was oblivious of everyone and everything (with the possible exception of the food bucket), but Babs was always at her best with a crowd to admire her; at these times the pool was never free of her and she would play to the gallery with all the ogling archness of a third-rate pantomime dame. Her great belly-flops in pursuit of bread scraps would send the water showering over the sleeping Sam until, in disgust, he would be forced to move to a less vulnerable portion of the cage.

Sam, strangely enough, did not seem to like the water. Even if food was thrown into the pool he would not go after it but would stand at the edge of the concrete and try to hook it out with his paw. If this failed he would ignore it. Twice, however, I sam him venture into the pool to play with his wife, and it was a sight worth watching. Babs on her own performed every action with a complete lack of humor; she had a set, intent look about her, as though she were performing something very objectionable but would do it whatever the cost. The only time I saw her look as though she was enjoying herself was on those occasions when Sam joined her in the water; only then did her expression seem pleasant and good-humored. Sam would sit waist-deep in the water and hug and bite his mate very gently, a benign kindliness shining from his eyes. Babs, on the other hand, would sometimes get so excited that she would bite him quite hard and he would be forced to admonish her with a skull-splitting slap. They would duck each other by the simple method of grabbing a mouthful of the loose skin of the neck and then sinking below the surface, dragging their mate with them. Their huge behinds would bob on the surface of the water like white pincushions while down in the green depths their forequarters would be slapping and biting in an ecstasy of high spirits. They would stay submerged for lengthy periods and then suddenly burst to the surface hissing and snorting, the water running right from their fur.

Babs was childlike in her wholehearted enjoyment of any toy that was given to her. Anything would do—an old motor tire, a log of wood, a tuft of grass or a bone. She preferred to have something that could be easily managed in the water and that would not sink too rapidly. One morning I inadvertently left a bucket in the cage after we had cleaned out and we did not notice it until we had let the bears out of the traps, by which time, of course, it was too late to do anything. We tried to retrap them so that we could remove the bucket, but they ignored our efforts. Sam, having assured himself that there was no food in it, took no further notice of it. Babs, being of a more boisterous nature, obviously regarded it as a gift from heaven, sent to relieve the monotony of captivity. She chivvied it around the rocks, banging it with one great paw, apparently enjoying the bloodcurdling screeches it produced as it grated on the cement. Eventually it rolled noisily down the slope into the pool, where it floated lopsidedly. Babs stood at the edge of the water trying to reach it with her paw, but it had floated too far away. At last she dived in after it, and the miniature tidal wave this action produced filled the bucket, which promptly sank into the green depths. Undaunted, Babs turned upside down and searched the bottom for it. In a minute or two she reappeared with the bucket hanging from her arm by its handle; she looked ludicrously like a milkmaid. Having recaptured her prize, she was not going to risk losing it again, so she lay on her back in the water with the bucket balanced on her stomach, patting it lovingly with her paws and occasionally tipping it up to sniff ponderously into the tinny, echoing interior.

After a time she grew careless again, and once more the bucket sank in a flurry of bubbles. She dived after it, and this time she reappeared wearing it like a hat, the handle under her chin, to the almost hysterical delight of Joe. She had some difficulty in removing it from her head, which gave us a few anxious moments, and this convinced her that the bucket could do with a lesson. Taking the handle in her mouth, she carried it out of the pool and dropped it on the concrete. With the air of one carrying out an absorbing experiment, she placed one paw on the side of the bucket and pressed. This simple, and apparently ineffectual, gesture made the bucket look as

though it had been caught beneath a pile driver; the sides were squashed in and the bottom bulged out like a blister. Having thus exhausted its possibilities, Babs lost interest in it and slouched off for a quiet swim.

Periodically Babs would be afflicted with a species of blind boil that would appear between the toes of her front foot. These were very worrying, as they took some time to burst and would cause her great pain. Joe would stand hunched over the barrier rail watching her limp round the cage, his face puckered with sorrow.

90

"Poor old thing, then," he would commiserate softly, "*Poor old girl.*"

We could do nothing except watch her painful progress round the cage until such time as the boil, bulged with its own poison, would burst and leave a smear of yellow pus on the white fur of her paw, a process which took two days. While her paw was swollen and throbbing Babs would never go into the pool, but as soon as it burst—almost before it had completely drained of pus—she would plunge back into the water.

On one occasion the boil did not burst on the second day as usual; on the third morning her paw was still swollen tight as a drum and we noticed that the swelling was spreading up her leg toward the elbow. This was serious, and so we went into action. We cajoled her into the traps and then gave her some M&B tablets crushed up and concealed in a piece of meat. Then we boiled a bucket of water on the little back stove in The Haven and mixed disinfectant with it. Our idea was to foment her paw in the hopes of bursting the boil, but Babs was not at all keen to participate in this scientific experiment. The traps were long, and as soon as we approached one end of them with the steaming bucket Babs would hastily hobble off to the other end. Eventually, with the aid of two planks, three forks and a spade, we got her cornered at one end, where she sat hissing like a steam engine and giving warning growls. Then we threw a splash of hot water over the swollen paw and Babs lifted it up quickly, hissing with rage and pain, and tried to break through the barrier of planks and forks. Luckily, these held; we threw some more water over her paw, and this time she only complained mildly. Gradually, as the warmth crept through her fur, she became

91

quieter, and eventually she lay down and closed her eyes. Before the bucket was empty the boil burst, spouting a stream of pus across the concrete, and Babs gave a sigh of relief. Two more buckets of water were used to clean away the matter as it dribbled from the shilling-sized hole in her paw. Half an hour later we let her out of the traps, and within a minute she was rolling and splashing in the pool as though there was nothing at all wrong with her.

Before working with Babs and Sam I had never considered that a polar bear could move with any speed, and so I was surprised, to say the least, when Babs proved that she could move with the alacrity of a tiger. The only time she demonstrated these bursts of speed was when she was sufficiently annoyed to make an attempt on one's life. Sam rarely hurried and never seemed to get dangerously annoyed; if he was ruffled he would let you know it by giving a warning hiss through protruded lips. Babs gave no warning and needed very little excuse to attack. The first time she gave me a demonstration of what she could do was one morning when she was in a foul temper for some reason known only to herself. She hissed and growled when we trapped them up so that we could clean out the cage, and when we let them out again she shambled around hissing and muttering to herself and growling at Sam if he ventured too close. She was at the far side of the cage when I accidentally kicked over a bucket, and the noise it made gave her something to focus her rage upon. She twisted round in a sudden spasm of anger and then charged toward me at a rolling gallop. This ended, when she reached the bars between us, in four enormous bounces, as though she were a giant ball; she covered the ground so quickly and with equal speed stuck her back-breaking paw through the bars that I only just stepped back in time. Disappointed at having missed me, she shambled off hissing to herself and went and sulked in the sun.

I should have been warned by this episode, but I was not, so it was not long afterward that Babs caught me bending. The space between the barrier rail and the bars of the polar-bear cage used to get littered with candy papers, cigarette packets, paper bags and other debris that the thoughtful public would drop there, and it was our job to clean this up. I went one afternoon to perform this duty and found Babs asleep at one end of the enclosure. I chose the end farthest from her, climbed over the barrier rail, and started to clean up. I became so absorbed in my task that I quite forgot to keep an eye on the bears. I was just bending down to pick up a piece of paper when there was a thud and a hiss behind me, and the next moment something caught my bottom a terrific clout. I was propelled forward like a hawking swallow and landed flat on my face in the rank grass. Rolling over, I found Babs sitting on her hind legs, leering at me in triumph. What amazed me was the fact that the bars of the cage were close together and so the only part of her paw that Babs could get through was her toes and long nails; yet, even so, she had managed to put enough force into the blow to knock me down. As I massaged myself tenderly I wondered what it would be like to be clouted by Babs if there were no bars between us. From the look in her eye I could tell that she would be only too willing to demonstrate this if I would let her.

Every other day or so, Jesse would be moved to deliver a short lecture on natural history to some member of the public. These never varied but were repeated over and over again, word for word, with monotonous regularity. They were repeated so often, in fact, that one or two of them had achieved a fame in the park that was almost legendary. Perhaps the best known of these was his discourse on polar bears, which nearly the entire keepering staff could repeat word for word. Sam had a habit, not uncommon in bears, which is called weaving. This consisted of standing in one spot, sometimes for as much as an hour, swaying his head and neck to and fro like a pendulum, his eyes fixed unseeingly on the distant horizon. The sight of this great white beast performing this strange action would provoke cries of delight and astonishment from the onlookers, and eventually one more misguided than the rest would look round for a keeper to explain the phenomenon. Jesse would appear at the knowledge seeker's elbow with a suddenness that was startling. Recovering from their surprise at his sudden appearance, which had an almost telepathic quality about it, the members of the public would require to know if it could be explained why the bear was swaying thus, to and fro.

"Well," Jesse would commence, fixing them with an earnest eye, "it's a long story, and even then I don't know if I'm right or not. . . ."

Here a pause; even with this modest phrasing he managed to convey the impression that he was never wrong. The public would produce cigarettes, and Jesse would lean on the barrier rail, puffing slowly.

"It's what they calls weaving," he would continue meditatively. "You gets it a lot in elephants. No one knows what they does it for, though some say this and some say that. *I* think the reason is *this* . . ."

94

Here he would take a deep breath and suck his teeth musically, prolonging the suspense.

"Polar bears, as I 'spect you know, comes from the South Pole, where it's all ice and snow and such. These bears feed on seals, and I believe they catch 'em with this weaving. They starts to weave on the edge of the ice, see? Along comes a seal and sees 'em and gets interested, see? He pokes his head up to have a look. And then—*wham!*—the bear's got him. I think it's a sort of hypnotism myself. Sort of fascinates the seal, d'you see?"

The curious thing about this is that during the many hundreds of times I heard Jesse deliver this lecture I never once heard a member of the public ask him if elephants weaved to catch seals also. Neither did they question the statement that polar bears came from the South Pole. But Jesse was always richer by a shilling at the end of his lecture.

Babs and Sam were an amusing and interesting pair of animals, and in watching their habits and characters I grew quite fond of them. Perhaps the most amusing episode that the polar bears participated in was the occasion when Babs was supposed to have a cub. It was, however, one of those episodes which are considered funny only afterward, not at the time.

The day's work being over, I was sitting in The Haven making myself a piece of toast on the fire when Joe, who had been walking round the section, appeared in the doorway looking very worried.

"Here," he said, with great mysteriousness, "come and look at this."

Reluctantly, I left my toast-making and followed him down

to the polar-bear cage. As far as I could see, everything looked normal.

"What's the matter, Joe?" I inquired.

"Can't you see?"

I looked round the cage again.

"No. What is it?"

"She's *bleeding!*" said Joe in a hoarse stage whisper, looking round furtively to see that we were not overhead.

"Who is?"

"Babs, of course. Who d'you think?"

I watched Babs, who was patrolling the bars, and at last made out a faint smudge of dried blood on her hind leg.

"Oh, yes, I can see it. On her hind leg."

"Shhh!" said Joe frantically. "D'you want everyone to hear?"

There was no one within two hundred yards of us, but Joe, as I mentioned before, was inclined to be hypersensitive about these matters.

"What do you think it is?" I asked. "Has she cut herself?"

"Come with me," Joe replied.

He led the way back to The Haven and we held a council of war behind closed doors.

"I think she's in cub," said Joe firmly.

"But, Joe, she isn't any bigger than she was," I protested.

"You can't tell with all that hair," said Joe darkly, as though Babs had concealed some disreputable secret from him.

"Well, what are we going to do? If she has a cub in there old Sam will eat it, sure as anything."

"We must get her into the traps," said Joe Napoleonically.

This was not so easily accomplished, for Babs had already been in the traps once that day and did not see why she should be locked up again. Sam, however, thinking there might be some food in it for him, came and sat in the traps hopefully and we had quite a job getting him out. At last Joe had to go to the other side of the cage and keep Sam there by feeding him bits of fat while I tried to tempt his wife into the traps. After half an hour we were successful and Babs was safely locked up, while her husband sat outside the traps on his huge behind, looking vastly interested in the whole business.

"Now," said Joe, "we must give her some bedding."

"Straw?" I suggested.

"Yes, let's get a bale from the Pit."

When I returned with the straw Joe was looking worried again.

"She's thirsty," he said. "It's too damned hot for her here. She gets no shade. We can't leave her like this."

"Let's cover the top of the trap with something," I suggested.

A search round The Haven produced an old door, and with considerable effort we hoisted this on top of the traps. This gave Babs some shade, but our actions had made her even more angry and she hissed and growled vigorously. Sam just sat there and watched us with rapt attention, clutching his tummy with huge paws.

"There!" said Joe, wiping the sweat from his face. "Now for the straw."

It was at this point that Sam began to take an active interest in the proceedings; as fast as we pushed the straw through the bars at one side of the trap he hooked it out through the bars at the other side, examining each bundle carefully, though whether for food or progeny we could not decide. We tried every way we could to stop him; we roared at him, rattled spades on the bars, threw lumps of fat at him, but it was no use.

"The damned old fool!" said Joe.

We were both hot and tired. Sam was sitting on a huge pile of straw, while his wife had only a few sprigs left in the traps.

"It's no good, Joe, he won't leave it alone. She'll just have to have the cub on the concrete, that's all."

"Yes," said Joe miserably, "I suppose she will."

So we left Sam shuffling in the straw and Babs looking very angry in the traps. That evening when the park closed Babs showed no signs of giving birth, so we left her shut up and went home.

Late that night I was wondering how Babs was getting on when it suddenly struck me that there was a perfectly natural explanation of the whole affair: Babs was in season. This sudden thought made me almost hysterical.

One look at Joe's face in the morning told me that he had thought of the same thing.

"Why the hell didn't we think of it?" he inquired bitterly. "What a pair of bloody fools, ay?"

Soon, however, he saw the funny side of it, and we were still laughing uproariously when we reached the polar-bear cage. Joe stopped laughing abruptly.

"Where's all the straw gone?" he asked in amazement.

A few sprigs adhered to Sam's shaggy coat, but that was all. The concrete was strawless, as though it had been swept.

"OOOooo!" wailed Joe suddenly, in awful anguish, "Just look at the pool! Oh, the dirty old swine!"

There was so much straw in the pool you could hardly see the water. Sam must have spent a very exciting and interesting night placing it there out of harm's way. Of course the waste pipe was throughly clogged; there is nothing quite like a bale of wet straw for blocking a waste pipe. It took us two days to clear the pool and the pipe of straw, and during that time the weather was gloriously hot, which was a great help.

"Cubs!" was Joe's only comment. "Next time she wants cubs she can bloody well have them in the den, like any other bear."

After I had been working on the section for several weeks, Jesse one morning, to my surprise, promoted me. We were sitting in The Haven, having completed our breakfast, and Jesse had carefully and slowly lighted his pipe. When it was squeaking and gurgling to his satisfaction, he fixed me with a basilisk stare.

"You're doing all right, son," he said. "You're working quite well."

"Thank you," I said, in some surprise.

"Tell you what I'll do, son," said Jesse, stabbing his pipestem at me. "I'll give you the upper 'alf of the section. They can be your responsibility, see?"

I was both flattered and delighted. To look after animals in conjunction with other people was interesting, but to be given full charge of a group of animals was a much more exciting prospect.

As soon as I could, I made my way up to the top end of the section and surveyed my domain. There was the modest-sized chalk pit in which lived Peter the wombat. Although I dutifully left bread, carrots and other tidbits in this enclosure every day, I had never actually met Peter, for he had constructed a series of burrows for himself in the bone-white chalk face and seemed to be an antisocial animal. I decided

I would have to get on intimate terms with him as soon as possible. Not far away, in a cage that was thoroughly over-grown with elder bushes, lived the group of five arctic foxes. Here again, I had not been able to do any more than dump the food into their cage and leave them to it. They were nervous creatures and required time and attention spent on winning their friendship. In the next enclosure, equally overgrown,

lived the raccoonlike dogs, curious, shaggy animals with fox-like faces, tails and bodies covered with a thick pelt of bear-like fur, and short little bowlegs which gave them the rolling gait of a drunken sailor.

I surveyed my new territory very carefully to see how I could improve things. The first thing I decided was that both the arctic-fox and the raccoonlike-dog cages were so overgrown that the animals were scarcely visible, so with the aid of a saw and a billhook I spent a happy and strenuous couple of hours cutting down the nettles and cutting back the elder bushes. By the time I had finished, the enclosures really looked quite respectable. The animals could now be seen, but they still had plenty of undergrowth left to hide in should they want to.

Then I tried to find out what particular food each of these three species was especially attracted to. I discovered, for example, that the arctic foxes doted on eggs. I found this out quite by accident, for I had come across a blackbird's egg which had fallen from the nest and was hardly cracked. I put it into the bucket I was carrying, meaning to give it to Sam to see if he would eat it, but as I passed the foxes' cage they were flitting round the door, having heard the clank of the bucket, and I threw the egg over the wire to them. It fell and split open, the yolk remaining unbroken but the white spattering over the ground. One of the foxes approached it carefully, sniffing through a maze of quivering whiskers; another joined it and then another. In a second they had all got the scent, and a vigorous fight broke out, more impressive because it was fought in complete silence. The fox who was busy lapping at the yolk was bitten in the hind leg, and he turned with bared teeth and floored his antagonist. Two more circled round the egg-bespattered earth, snapping and paw-lifting at each other. Another of them had got the whole thing down to a fine art and he kept darting into the fight, snapping and licking almost in the same movement; then he would sit down and lick his lips carefully before rushing in again. Soon every patch of dampness had been licked up and they all fell to licking their lips and sniffing each other's noses hopefully. As I moved on down the path they followed me with eager chrysanthemum-brown eyes, hoping for another egg to appear from the pail. After that, I used to go to a hedge that bordered a farm I knew of and pinch chickens' eggs for my foxes. In consequence of this they soon became quite tame and no

101

longer did their hysterical silent circling of the outer perimeter of the cage when I was cleaning up inside.

The almost complete silence of these foxes was something which puzzled me considerably. I say *almost* complete silence, for it was only once that I heard them make any sound and this was so curious and beautiful that I wish I could have heard it again—a thing one cannot say about all animal noises. One morning I approached the pine wood which sheltered the foxes' enclosure and I was attracted by a strange sound, shrill and whewling, like a flock of sea gulls. There were no birds in the trees above, and I did not think that the noise emanated from the raccoonlike dogs, whose cage I had just passed. The sound continued, rising and falling, sometimes seeming near at hand and then as though it were a distant echo brought by the wind. To my surprise, when I reached the foxes' enclosure I found that they were the authors of this strange song. They stood in a circle about the door, fragile legs straddled, golden eyes expressionless, heads thrown back, with open mouths, and this extraordinary noise was being brought forth in little gusts, wild and birdlike. I could not think why they had broken their silence in this way, for, as I say, normally they were as loquacious as Trappist monks. They showed no more than their normal interest in the food, and I could never work out what had brought on this sudden beautiful chorus.

After reading that an Arctic expedition in 1875 had discovered that arctic foxes laid up stores of dead lemmings hidden in crannies in the rocks as a provision for the long Arctic nights during which they would obtain little, if any, food, I was anxious to find out if my foxes did the same. Up till then they had shown no signs of hoarding their meat. This I knew, as I had searched diligently among the twisted elder roots and under the dead leaves. But then, when the cold weather came upon us, one morning I discovered a chunk of meat half hidden beneath a drift of dead leaves. It was quite fresh, but a further search revealed no less than five slices of meat, some purple with rot, hidden cunningly in various parts of the cage. I was forced to remove them for purely hygienic reasons, but the foxes continued to build up little stores as long as the cold weather lasted.

The raccoonlike dogs I managed to make friends with more quickly, since they were all gluttons by profession. The older female, though she got to the point of taking food from my hand, would never allow me to take liberties with her, but her daughter, I discovered, was bubbling over with love for the human being, providing he had some food with which to fill the permanently aching void in her stomach. Her name, a corruption of goodness knows what, was Wops, and very soon I had only to go the wire and shout for her and she would come waddling out of the bushes, her eyes bright in her alert little face. It was a little annoying to realize that it was for the meat in my hand that she came running and not for the purpose of the convivial chat. However, in case I should think she were ungracious, she always stopped a minute when the meat was gone.

At first glance, she was very badgerlike, with her black and white face markings and the same rolling waddle, but she was much larger and her bushy tail was almost the size of her body. On her face, as I say, the fur was marked with black and white, but on her body, legs and tail there was a brindle mixture of deep brown, reddish and gray hairs. These hairs were very long and silky. In Japan, where the raccoonlike dogs are found in the wilds, the skins are apparently much sought after for clothing. The meat is also considered a delicacy, but I felt that Wops was far too charming to skin and eat.

In the wild state this animal is chiefly nocturnal, and this was certainly true of Wop's parents. They could only be tempted out during the daytime with heavy bribes of food, but Wops would always be ready, waddling round through the bushes hoping that somebody would happen along with something to eat. It could be safely said of her that she lived to eat rather than she ate to live. Her affections were entirely guided by her stomach. This was a good thing from my point of view, for if she had not had this obsession about food I could not have had such long conversations with her or watched her so closely. These gastronomic tributes she considered her due, and I gave them gladly while contemplating her appetite with grave misgivings, for her girth almost exceeded her length.

Only once did Wops turn on the hand that fed her. That the hand—or, rather, the leg—belonged to me was unfortunate but entirely my own fault. I had taken a small group of people down to her cage in order to show her off to them. After feeding her through the wire for some time I thought that I would add some variety by going in and picking her up for closer inspection. The fact that my audience included a remarkably pretty girl, I still maintain, had nothing to do with my action. As I entered, Wops regarded me with suspicion, for she knew that I joined her in the cage in order to clean out every morning. That I should join her in captivity twice in one day was too much to ask even of her. Quickly accepting the last bit of meat from my hand, she started toward me with a preoccupied air. Finding that I would not move from her path in order that she might attain the peace and quiet of her hut, she walked up to me and with a sideways chop of her jaws left a neat visiting card of teethmarks on my shin. Cries of horror came from the audience outside the cage. Wops stood at my feet and looked up into my face belligerently. She was not being vicious, that I knew. It was just that I would not get out of her way and she was telling me as plainly as possible that she wanted to pass. It was her cage, she implied, and by God she was going to show me who the owner was.

I had no meat left with which to bribe her, and retreat was impossible with the audience outside—my public, as it were. Neither could we stand there indefinitely staring at each other. I felt desperately in my pockets and with great pleasure discovered a very elderly and dirty date, one of a handful I had filched from the stores that morning. With this hairy relic I knew I could do anything I wanted with Wops, for of all foodstuffs dates were her special weakness. She accepted it with every symptom of delight, and while her attention was occupied in eating it I picked her up quickly and walked to the wire with her. Keeping my face well away from her jaws, I explained her antisocial conduct to the audience by saying that she was a little off color that week, accompanying this outrageous fabrication with a look of becoming modesty. This had the effect of embarrassing everybody except Wops and me; a few of the younger audience were led hurriedly away to forestall questions. Wops was extraordinarily heavy, so I replaced her on the ground. There she shook herself like a dog, sniffed round hopefully to see if there was another date and, finding that there was not, heaved a reproachful sigh and waddled off.

Wops, toward winter, grew a tremendously thick coat and

her tail assumed twice its normal proportions, but she never showed any signs of wanting to hibernate, a habit which in the wild state makes these creatures unique in the dog family. She did grow a little more lethargic and show a disinclination to come out of her hut when there was snow on the ground, but that was all. Although I could find no reference to these animals building nests to hibernate in, Wops did something which may have been an attempt to build a nest. I noticed one morning that she had been very busy among the bushes in her cage. There were branches and leaves, freshly broken, littering the ground when I went in. After my normal tribute of food to her I sat and watched her for some considerable time before she suddenly stopped trotting about and started breaking branches. She went into her hut and after a moment or so came out again and then peered around into the branches above her. Selecting a twig which was hanging within reach, she grasped it in her mouth and pulled hard, all four fat legs braced against the ground. When she had wrenched it off she proceeded to carry it about the cage in an aimless fashion, occasionally tripping over it. At last she tired of it and dropped it on the ground and then started to search for a new one. While I watched she broke three twigs and treated each one in the same way; then she returned to her hut for a snooze. It seemed as though she was trying to accomplish something, but something which eluded her memory at the last moment. I never found any twigs inside her hut, but this may have been due to the fact that it was small and Wops was so fat that there was room only for her inside it.

Whilst, as I say, I met with a certain success in gaining the confidence of the racoonlike dogs and the arctic foxes, Peter the wombat still remained elusive. By trying out a selection of foods I discovered that he, like Wops, had a passion for dates. So one day I deliberately delayed feeding him until the late evening. When I got to his enclosure I found that altering his timetable had had the desired effect, for he was standing by the wire looking forlorn and lost, like a teddy bear in search of a nursery. He was a most attractive little animal, standing about one foot six in height, with a round, compact body that made him look very bearlike. His hindquarters sloped down suddenly and his legs were short and stubby and turned inward; his face was very similar to that of a koala bear except that the latter's eyes are large and fringed with fur while Peter's were small and set close to his head. He had, however, the same egg-shaped patch of skin on his nose covered with sparse bristles, and his eyes were round and black like the koala's. The main difference, I felt, was in the

107

expression: the koala looks—even if it is not—alert and questioning, whereas Peter looked dazed and bewildered. Quite frankly, he looked as though someone had just hit him on the head with a brick. His fur was a nice shade of gray, paling a bit toward his stomach—the nice cool gray of a wood pigeon. To my surprise, he made no fuss when I entered the cage, and came forward quite readily to take dates from my hand, but he would not let me touch him, and having eaten his fill, he waddled off and wedged himself into his burrow in the chalk. After that, he would come out every day at mealtime, accept food from my hand and then disappear back into his burrow.

Since the chalk pit he inhabited was on a slope of the Downs, the mouth of his burrow had to face the direction from which we got our worst weather, but Peter had evolved a novel and interesting method of keeping his bedroom dry. His tunnel was some four feet long and ended in a small circular chamber. Peter would shuffle into this and, as the diameter was exact, his bottom blocked the mouth of this bedroom as though it were a door. So he stayed, letting snow, wind and rain blow up the tunnel, keeping warm and dry by presenting the least vulnerable part of his anatomy to the inclemencies of the weather. Once he was wedged in like that, with his claws embedded in the chalk, it would have taken a gang of men with spades to dislodge him, so his action was twofold: it protected him not only from the weather but also from any enemies that might creep down the tunnel in pursuit of him. Both disturbances would meet the furry, hard buttocks, on which they would leave little impression.

It was the day that Jesse put me in charge of my own

animals that I was due to go to the Beales' for dinner. Needless to say, Mrs. Bailey took the news of my promotion with equanimity; she was much more concerned with what I was going to wear to the Beales', for she treated my invitation rather as though it were a summons to Buckingham Palace.

"And," I said triumphantly over tea, "I'm sure that eventually I can get those foxes to eat out of my hand."

"Fancy," said Mrs. Bailey, not listening. "I've darned your blue socks. I've decided that you're to wear your blue shirt; it goes nicely with your eyes."

"Thank you," I said. "You see, this wombat will be a bit of a problem . . ."

"And your clean hankies are in the left-hand drawer. I'm only sorry you haven't a blue one."

"Leave the boy alone, can't you?" said Charlie mildly. "He's not entering a beauty contest."

"That's not the point, Charlie Bailey, as well you know. This might lead to things. The boy must look nice. Apart from anything else, what would people say if I let him go out looking like a gypsy? They'd say I was letting him go to the dogs. They'd say I was taking his money under false pretenses. He comes here, away from his mother and home, away from people who can guide him—well, it's up to us. And you may do as you wish, Charlie Bailey, but I for one am going to see that the boy goes out clean and decent and a credit to himself and us. How would it be if Captain Beale . . ."

"What were you saying about wombats, boy?" said Charlie, turning his back on this flood.

Eventually, after I had washed, shaved, cleaned my teeth, dressed and been inspected by Mrs. Bailey with a fiercely critical eye, as though I were a guardsman about to take part in the trooping of the color, I was allowed to go.

On my arrival at the Beales' the door was opened for me by Mrs. Beale, who was looking pale and harassed. I discovered she always looked pale and harassed when the captain was cooking.

"Good evening, Gerry," she said. "So glad you could come. Do go into the drawing room. Billy and the girls are there and Billy will give you a drink."

The hall was redolent with the smell of curry. From the direction of the kitchen came a sound like a trainload of copper pans falling over a cliff. Mrs. Beale winced.

"Gladys! *Gladys!*" roared Captain Beale from behind the kitchen door. It sounded as though he were thrashing about waist-deep in broken china. *"Gladys!"*

"What's the—matter, William?" called Mrs. Beale.

"The salt! Where the hell's the salt? Why do people always move things when I'm cooking? Where's the bloody salt?"

"I'm coming, dear," said Mrs. Beale, giving me a long-suffering smile. "Go into the drawing room, Gerry, I won't be a minute."

In the drawing room I found Laura, Billy's sister, and the two plump European refugees who, having escaped from the Continent earlier in the war, were now billeted with the Beales. Billy was pouring beer into a glass as I entered.

"Hello, have a drink," he said grinning. "Dad's cooking— did you hear him?"

"Yes," I said, "it smells delicious."

We sat in the drawing room making desultory conversation while the sounds of Captain Beale's culinary activities were wafted to us like the sounds of a fifteenth-century battle with plenty of armor. There would be a prolonged crash and rattle reminiscent of sixteen knights falling off their horses simultaneously, and then the captain's voice.

"Coriander! No, no, the brown jar! Now—chili. Where's the chili? Oh. Yes. Well, *I* didn't put it there. Hot? Too hot? What do you mean, too hot? Of course it's not too hot—it's not bloody hot enough! I'm not swearing. More coriander! *Now look what you've done*—you've left the *rice* boil over."

Eventually the captain and Mrs. Beale appeared. She was still looking harassed, whereas the captain, his face scarlet and perspiring, had the righteous and self-satisfied air of one who had vanquished a particularly malevolent and recalcitrant foe.

"Ah, Durrell," he greeted me. "Just been cooking."

"He heard you," said Billy.

"It smells delicious," I said hastily.

"Not bad, not bad," said the captain, gulping his beer thirstily. "A good hot one this time. Curries are like women, Durrell. Some mild, some hot—never can tell until you . . . er . . . er . . . um . . . um . . ."

"William, dear!" said Mrs. Beale quellingly. "Come along, girls, let's go and lay the table."

Presently, the table laid, we trooped into the dining room and the first course was served: great bowls of mulligatawny soup, the virulent yellow of a jaundice epidemic and of a piquancy that left you feeling faintly surprised that your lips did not burst into flame.

At this point Captain Beale took from his pocket a large red handkerchief and draped it over his bald head so that the edge hung down as far as his eyes. It made him look like a particularly bloodthirsty pirate.

111

"I wish you wouldn't do that, William," said Mrs. Beale. "What will Gerry think?"

"Think? Think?" said the captain, glaring out from under his handkerchief. "He'll think I know what's bloody what. Sops up the sweat—always used to do it on the Coast. Had a towel there, Durrell, d'you see? What with the temperature in the tropics and the curry, you get a real good sweat on. Sweat horse troughs. Sit there in the evening, nice pink gin —sit there, mother-naked, with a curry and a towel and have a good sweat."

"William, dear."

"Of course, you weren't mother-naked when you had guests," explained the captain hastily. "No, no, with guests you wore underpants."

Eventually, the last searing spoonful of soup had been imbibed and the captain lumbered out into the kitchen and reappeared bearing a monstrous tureen.

"Can't get enough meat for a decent curry with this damned rationing," he grumbled, "so you'll have to put up with this. This is rabbit."

He removed the lid of the tureen, and a cloud of curry-scented steam enveloped the table like a London fog. It seized hold of your throat with a hard, cunning Oriental grasp and built up in thick layers in your lung cavities. We all coughed furtively. The curry was delicious, but I thanked heaven that I came from a household which specialized in hot dishes; otherwise, my tongue and vocal chords would never have survived the captain's rabbit curry. After the first few mouthfuls everyone, larynx shriveled and twisted, was mouthing incoherently and grasping at the water jug like a drowning man at a straw.

"Don't drink water!" roared the captain, the sweat pouring in cascades down his face, his spectacles misting with the heat. "Water makes it worse."

"I told you that you were making it too hot, William, dear," remonstrated Mrs. Beale, her face scarlet.

The two refugees were making strange, unintelligible Middle European noises, Billy's face was the color of his hair, and Laura's normally pale face was congested.

"Nonsense," said the captain, mopping his head, face and neck with his handkerchief and undoing his shirt down to the waist, "it's not too hot. Just a decent heat, eh, Durrell?"

"Well, it's all right for me, sir," I said, "but I can imagine it would be a little too hot for some people."

"Fiddy faddy!" said the captain, waving a spade-shaped hand in dismissal. People don't know what's good for them."

"It can't be good for you to have it *this* hot," said Mrs. Beale in a strangled voice, gulping water.

"Of course it is," roared the captain belligerently, glaring at her through misty spectacles. "It's a well-known medical *fact* that hot curry is good for you."

"But not this hot, dear, surely?"

"Of course *this* hot. And *this* is not hot. This is a namby-pamby curry compared to what I *could* have made."

An involuntary shudder ran round the table at the thought of what the captain could have made.

"Why, on the Coast," the captain went on, shoveling curry into his mouth, "we had curry so hot that it was like swallering *red-hot coals.*"

He beamed at us triumphantly and did a rapid mopping-up operation on his face and head.

"It can't be good for one," said Mrs. Beale, clinging to her original premise.

"Of course it is, Gladys!" said the captain impatiently. "Why do you think curry was invented in the tropics, hm? To burn out disease. That's why. Why d'you think I never got beriberi or yaws, eh? Why d'you think I never fell to bits with leprosy?"

"William, dear!"

"Well, it's true," said the captain truculently. "All due to curry. Goes in one end and comes out the other—burns you right through. Sort of cauterizes you, d'you see?"

"William, *please*."

"All right, all right," the captain rumbled, "but I don't know what's the matter with you all. I make you a decent curry and you all carry on as if I'd tried to kill you! If you had a curry like this every day you wouldn't get colds in the winter."

Here, I must say, I was inclined to agree with the captain. With one's body incandescent with his curry, one felt that the humble cold germ would not stand a chance. As it was, as I walked home that night over the dark common I felt I ought to be leaving a coruscating trail of curry glowing behind me like the tail of a comet.

Apparently the fact that I could face his curry with equanimity endeared me to the captain, and so, after that, every Thursday I went to dinner at the Beales', and very pleasant evenings they were for me.

CHAPTER 5

A Gallivant of Gnus

———◆———

Indulge the loud unseemly jape and
never brush their hair.
   —BELLOC, *Bad Child's Book of Beasts*

AFTER I had been working for a couple of months on the lions, Phil Bates met me one morning and told me that he wanted me to start on a new section. I was delighted; not that I was not happily ensconced on the lions and working very happily with Jesse and Joe, but I had, after all, come to Whipsnade to obtain experience and so the more sections I worked on, the more scope it would give me. My new section was known as "the bears." It contained, as its name implied, all the large bumbling, biscuit-colored brown bears in the Whipsnade collection, together with a giant paddock full of zebras and herds of gnus and other antelopes, ending up with the small fry in the shape of wolves and warthogs.

The section was run by one Harry Rance, a diminutive, stocky individual with a broken nose and a pair of twinkling gentian-blue eyes. I found him sitting in a small room behind the zebra sheds, sipping meditatively at a large battered tin mug of cocoa and whittling at a hazel twig.

" 'Lo, boy," he greeted me, "I hear you're working along with me."

117

"Yes," I said. "I'm glad they've shifted me to this section, because you've got a lot of nice stuff."

"Nice enough stuff, boy," he said, "but you want to watch it. Most of that stuff you've been dealing with on the lions you didn't go in with; with our stuff you've gotta go in with it, so you'll have to watch your step. They can look tame enough, but they can catch you bending."

He jerked his thumb at a stall where a fat dazzling black-and-white zebra stallion was standing placidly chewing at a wisp of hay.

"Take 'im," said Harry. "Looks as calm as a baby, doesn't 'e?"

I examined the zebra carefully. He reminded me of nothing more or less than a rather outsized, overweight donkey that someone had got at with a couple of pots of paint. I felt it would be the work of a moment to slip into the stall and saddle him up.

"Just go up to the stall," said Harry.

I walked up to the stall, and the zebra swung his head round and focused his ears on me. I walked a little closer and his nostrils widened into black velvety pools as he absorbed my scent. I moved still closer and still he made no move.

"He looks tame enough," I began, glancing at Harry.

The moment my eyes had switched away from the stallion he tucked in his backside and, in a sudden spurt, reached the stall door in a vicious machine-gun-like rattle of hoofs. He struck at me through the bars with open mouth, showing great, sharp, square yellow teeth. I leaped back so quickly that I fell over a bucket. Harry sat on his chair with his toes twisted round the legs, whittling away at his stick and chuckling silently to himself.

"See what I mean, boy?" he said as I picked myself up. "Calm as a baby, and a right bastard."

The first few days, as usual, were spent in learning the routine chores, the feeding times of the different animals and the proportions of food that you gave each one. Probably the hardest work on the section was our weekly mucking-out of the great buffalo shed. The herd had a vast acreage of sloping downland to wander in, surrounded by a tall iron fence, but they came up to the great low shed on the crest of the Downs to be fed every day. Normally we emptied the food through the fence, making piles of bran, crushed linseed cake, and oats, and then when the buffaloes had finished this we would pitchfork dozens of mangolds over the fence so they bounced and rolled, and the buffaloes moved with heavy enthusiasm after them, sinking their teeth into the crisp round bulbs with a noise like somebody splitting firewood. The apportioning of the oats and cake had to be done with care so that the older males did not get more than their fair share. The art of this was, I soon learned, to put out five or six piles, just sufficient in quantity to keep the males fully occupied for four or five minutes; then you could move farther down the fence and make further piles of food which the cows and calves could eat in peace without getting a horn up their rump.

Seen close to, the North American buffalo is, I think, one of the most impressive of all the cloven-hoofed animals. The massive, humped shoulders covered with a thick curly mane of fur, the plus-fours of fur round the stocky front legs, the curly wig on the great skull with the Viking horns curving out of it, give an immense sense of power. For the most part they moved slowly and ponderously, but they could butt each

other suddenly and savagely, swinging the great head like a battering ram. That they could move fast when they cared to I saw one day when a lorry that had been delivering a load of mangolds to the shed backfired as it was leaving. The herd, which had been clustered along the edge of the fence like a great chocolate-colored cumulus of curls, turned as one animal and thundered away over the green turf of the Downs at an incredible speed, kicking up chips of chalk as their hoofs bit deeply into the ground. They looked like some enormous and rather terrifying avalanche tumbling down the green slope of the Downs, and I would have hated to be in their way.

So when it came to the job of mucking out their shed I was always filled with a certain misgiving, for, as we forked up the straw and dung and piled it into barrows and wheeled it

out of the shed the old bulls of the herd (who never appeared
to tire of watching this performance) would come and stand
in a massive row in front of the open side of the shed and stare
at us with deep interest, occasionally uttering a prolonged,
sonorous snort which would make us jump. One day, one of
the old bulls suddenly lumbered into the shed amongst us and
we dropped our tools and fled incontinently. But we soon saw
that his invasion of the shed had not been with vicious intent;
he had merely spotted half a mangold which our cleaning
efforts had uncovered in his straw, and, having munched it
up, he lumbered out onto the Downs again.

On the southern slopes of their enclosure there was the
favorite rolling ground of the herd, and here their heavy
bodies had worn away the turf and left several great naked

patches of chalk, white against the green. To this rolling patch the old bulls would descend in a slow-moving, orderly line. Then they would lower themselves onto the chalk, and with vigorous kicks from their hind legs they would tumble their massive bodies onto their backs in a series of convulsive heaves. From a distance they looked as though they were trying to extricate themselves from an invisible net in which they had become entangled. The rough chalk rasped against their hides and removed the loose coat which always seemed to worry them. Presently, sufficiently relieved after half an hour or so of delicious scratching, they would scramble heavily to their feet and a convulsive quiver would travel over the soft brown skin on their flanks and belly, shaking off the loose chalk. Then they would lumber away to browse, with just a few white chips of chalk embedded in the tangled curls of their forequarters. When they were losing their winter coats the process appeared to drive them mad, and everywhere you looked the buffaloes would be leaning against the fence or against the gnarled hawthorn trunks, scratching and scratching, their eyes closed in a sort of ecstasy. I discovered that they employed another method to get rid of the loose hair round their heads and shoulders. The tiny, close-growing copses of the blackthorn trees provided excellent posts to scratch an irritating back, but their tightly interlaced branches hanging low to the ground were used by the buffaloes as a comb, for it provided a way of shearing off the dead winter coat. You would see them taking turns, walking deliberately under the trees so that the branches caught their thick manes and the thorns and twigs tore loose the dead hair. In the spring the blackthorn trees looked as though they were bearing a crop of some strange fruit, with all the tufts and sprigs of soft, fallow-colored hair hanging from their branches. These handfuls of soft fur would be eagerly sought out by the sparrows and yellowhammers to use as nest lining.

When the Europeans came to North America the buffaloes were almost as numerous as the stars. The great herds numbered in millions and were the biggest conglomeration of land mammals that the world has ever seen. To the Indian, the buffalo was everything—a house, food, clothing, even down to providing such mundane objects as needle and thread. But the Indian killed only what he could conveniently use, and his depredations had no effect on the countless thousands of these great shaggy animals. But with the coming of the European and his sophisticated weapons the picture changed. The buffalo was hunted murderously and slaughtered by the thousands. To begin with, the whole carcass was utilized, but then it palled as a source of food. Now they were killed in the same vast quantities, but for only two reasons: firstly, so that their tongues could be procured as a delicacy, and, secondly, as a deliberate policy of extermination, for it was felt that since the Indian relied so much on the buffalo, if the buffalo became extinct so would the Indian.

At this time professional buffalo hunters made their money and their reputations—people like Buffalo Bill Cody, whose biggest day's bag was two hundred and fifty of the great beasts. As the railroad proceeded across the prairie, cutting the buffalo's migrating roads, the animals were shot from the trains and left to rot. In places the stench from their rotting carcasses was so great that trains passing through this huge charnelhouse had to keep their windows up. With such hideous and profligate slaughter it is small wonder that in 1889 the buffalo, from being the most numerous land mammal ever recorded, dwindled to a scant five hundred specimens. Only then did a small cluster of conservation-minded people, horrified at the thought that the buffalo might vanish forever, take steps to ensure its survival. Now there are several thousand buffaloes in existence and the species is safe, but never again will mankind enjoy the awe-inspiring sight of the prairie covered as far as the eye can see in all directions by a black, moving rug of buffaloes.

Another animal we had on this section which is at the moment undergoing the same fate as the buffalo was the anoa. These are diminutive black buffaloes from the Celebes. They seemed terribly small—about the size of a Shetland pony—to be relatives of the great buffalo. They were quite little animals with long, earnest faces and soulful eyes; their dark fur was harsh to the touch and unevenly distributed over their fat rumps so that the dark, mauvey-pink skin showed through; their hoofs were small and neat and their alert ears delicately furred inside; their horns, some eight inches long, were absolutely straight and sharply pointed. The two that we had seemed very inoffensive; they would nuzzle bran from my hands and gaze up into my face with expressions of martyred innocence. It came as quite a surprise, when I read them up, to learn that they could be very dangerous indeed. Their small size, speed of movement, maneuverability and sharp horns had made them an animal to be reckoned with. It was because of their ferocity when disturbed that the anoas were left strictly alone by the local people in the Celebes for many years. But then, with the coming of modern weapons—particularly that absolutely indispensable one for every sportsman, the machine gun—the anoas' days became numbered, and now their outlook is very bleak.

The Chapman zebras, on the whole, I found to be very dull animals. They formed an attractive pattern against the grass of their vast enclosure but appeared to do nothing of interest except graze and occasionally have little bickering fights with each other, when, with ears back and teeth bared, they would threaten each other. The stallions, to a man, as it were, were determined to try and kill you, and as they could move with ferocious speed you always had to be on your guard.

First thing every morning, Harry and I would climb the fence into the zebra paddock and collect the velvety, dew-drenched crop of mushrooms that had sprouted there in the night. These Harry would cook in butter in a little saucepan, and we would devour them for our elevenses. They made a delicious meal, but the hazards involved in mushroom collecting with a couple of murderous zebra stallions in the paddock with you were extreme to say the least. We worked close together, with a pitchfork handy, and when one was bending down to pick mushrooms the other was watching the zebras. One morning there was particularly fine crop and we had filled half a bucket and were congratulating ourselves upon the enormous feed we should be able to have at eleven o'clock. I was just bending down to pick up an exceptionally succulent mushroom when Harry shouted, "Watch out, boy! The bastard's coming!"

I looked up and the zebra stallion was thundering toward me, his ears back, his lip pulled back over his yellow teeth. Leaving the bucket, I followed Harry's example and ran like a hare. We scrambled over the fence, panting and laughing. The zebra scudded to a halt by the bucket and glared at us, snorting indignantly. Then, to our extreme annoyance, he

125

swiveled round and with immense accuracy kicked the bucket in a great swooping parabola through the air, scattering white mushrooms like a comet's tail. It took us half an hour to collect the mushrooms again.

There was one zebra, however, that I did like. This was a solitary male gravvy. These are the biggest of all the zebras, and their body shape is more like a horse; their head is very long and elegant, and though it bears a superficial resemblance to a donkey's head it is really more like that of an Arab stallion, with a fine, delicate, velvety muzzle. The stripes are quite thin and very regular, as though drawn with a ruler, and the ears are enormous, like huge furry arum lilies. This particular zebra was, as far as I know, the only one of its kind in England, and, apart from its beauty and gentleness of disposition, its rarity entitled me to give it extra rations of crushed oats, which it would take delicately from my hand with lips that were as soft as the mushroom tops that grew in its paddock.

To the north of the section lay a large, green, velvety paddock surrounded by a crisp green crinoline of oak trees. Here lived what were undoubtedly the rarest animals in our care, a pair of young Père David deer. To look at, they were not nearly so graceful as, say, the red deer or fallow deer that lived not far away from them. By deer standards one would almost have called them ungainly. They stood some four foot high at the shoulder and they had long, earnest faces with curiously slanted, almond-shaped eyes. Under each eye there was a curious vent, a little pocket of pink skin which could open and close at will, which led nowhere and seemed to fulfill no useful purpose. They had stocky, rather donkeylike bodies; their color was a peculiar acorn-brown, with white bellies and a heart-shaped patch on their bottoms. To watch the Père David deer sauntering round their paddock, with the application of a little imagination you could place them. The shape and slant of the eyes, the curious body, the long black hoofs and—unique in the deer family—a long tufted tail like a donkey, all went to make them look as though they had wandered out of a rather uncertain Chinese print. Their movements were clumsy, lacking in the grace that is usually displayed by their family. Occasionally when I passed their paddock my sudden appearance would startle them and they would wheel round to face me, legs spread out, ears pricked; then they would set off in panic-stricken flight to the other end of their domain with a gait reminiscent of a drunken donkey. The legs seemed to be held very stiffly and the abnormal length of the body made the whole deer roll from side to side. When you compared it to the beautiful movements of the other deer you realized just how donkeylike the Père David was. The only part of it that had any of the normal beauty of line and movement of the deer family was the head and neck.

The story of the discovery and subsequent survival of this odd-looking deer is as curious as any in the annals of natural history. In the middle 1800s Père Armand David, a French missionary, worked and traveled in China, and, like so many men of the church in those days, he took a deep interest in natural history. I suspect, in fact, that the number of unique natural-history specimens he obtained greatly outnumbered the souls that he saved during his sojourn in China. It was he, in fact, who first obtained specimens of the now famous giant panda. While in Peking he heard a rumor to the effect that in the royal gardens of the Emperor's palace there existed a herd of deer—a type of deer, it was said, unknown anywhere else in China. This naturally intrigued Father David, but the problem was how to get a chance of seeing these animals. They were in a walled garden carefully guarded by Tatars; and at that time, of course, foreigners were scarcely tolerated in China, so Père David had to move with great caution. It shows the depth of the interest that the man had in natural history that he was prepared to take risks that could well have led to imprisonment or even death. His first step was to bribe a Tatar guard on the gate of the royal palace to allow him to climb up on top of the wall and survey the garden. From this vantage point he could see eventually a herd of deer feeding among the trees. It must have been a thrilling moment for him as he found himself looking at a herd of deer grazing about a hundred yards away and realized that he was seeing not only a new species but a particularly unusual one.

He at once wrote home to Paris, to Professor Milne-Edwards at the Museum of Natural History, describing his discovery:

> Three miles to the south of Peking there is a vast Imperial Park about thirty-six miles perhaps all round. There it is that since time immemorial deer and antelopes have lived in peace. No European can get into this park, but this spring, from the top of the surrounding wall, I had the good fortune to see, rather far off, a herd of more than a hundred of these animals, which looked to me like elks. Unfortunately, they had no antlers at this time; what characterizes the animal that I saw is the length of the tail, which struck me as being comparatively as long as the tail of the donkey, a feature not to be found in any of the cervides that I know. It is also smaller than the northern elk. I have made fruitless attempts to get the skin of this species. It is quite impossible to have even portions, and the French Legation feels incapable of managing to procure this curious animal by unofficial approaches to the Chinese Government. Luckily, I know some Tatar soldiers who are going to do guard duty in this park and I am sure, by means of a bribe, that I shall get hold of a few skins, which I shall hasten to send you. The Chinese give to this animal the name of Mi-Lou, which means the four odd features, because they consider that this deer takes after the stag by its antlers, the cow by its hoofs, the camel by its neck and the mule or even the donkey by its tail. . . .

Shortly afterwards a secret meeting was arranged with the Tatar soldiers, and one night the skin and bones of a male and a female were passed over the park wall. Père David lost no time in despatching these to Milne-Edwards. Over the next few years, through the efforts of the British envoy and the French Chargé d'Affaires, a number of live specimens were obtained. Most of these reached Europe safely, so that by

1870 the species were represented at several European zoos.

Little is known of the history of Père David's deer up to 1865, and the origin of the Peking herd is a complete mystery. As a wild animal, it is now believed to have been extinct two or three thousand years ago. Semi-fossil remains show that before this time it apparently roamed wild about the Honan district of China. There are no records to show whether the Peking herd had been maintained through all those centuries, or whether it had been founded more recently from other captive herds through which the species had been preserved. Chinese historical literature offers no help, because there is a complete confusion between Père David's deer and the reindeer. All that is certain is that by 1865 the Peking animals represented the sole survivors of the species.

He was now determined to obtain specimens, but this was not so easily done. He knew that, in spite of the penalty for such an action being death, sometimes the Tatar guards fed on poached venison, so with the aid of more bribes he succeeded in getting them to agree to save for him the skins and skulls of the next ones that they ate. In due course this was done and Père David shipped the skins and skulls back to the Museum of Natural History in Paris, where it was discovered that they were indeed a species new to science. In recognition of Father David's great contribution to Oriental natural history they were named *Elaphurus davidianus* in his honor.

Naturally, zoological gardens and private collections in Europe wanted to obtain specimens of this rare deer, and, indeed, if any deer could be called rare, Père David's could, for the only known living herd was in the Imperial Palace Gardens, and there is still a certain amount of doubt as to where they came from in the first place. It is almost as though they had evolved within the grounds of the Emperor's summer palace. The Chinese authorities, however, were not anxious for any of their national treasures to be exported, but at length, after prolonged negotiations, several pairs of the deer were sent to various zoos in Europe and a pair was sent to the then Duke of Bedford's extraordinary private menagerie at Woburn.

Not long after this the Yangtze River flooded its banks and the flood waters breached the wall round the Imperial Palace Gardens in several places. Most of the deer escaped into the surrounding countryside, where of course they were immediately slaughtered by the starving peasantry. There still remained, however, a tiny nucleus in the gardens; but it seemed that the Père David deer was dogged by bad luck, for next came the Boxer Rebellion and during this time the Tatar guards seized the opportunity of eating the remaining deer. So now the species was extinct in its home of origin and the total world population consisted of animals scattered about Europe.

The Duke of Bedford, one of the earliest and most intelligent conservationists, decided that he must add to his tiny herd at Woburn if the species was to be saved, so he negotiated with the zoological gardens that had specimens of the deer and eventually managed to establish a herd of eighteen. This was the total world population. Gradually, living under ideal conditions at Woburn, the animals increased in number until, at the time I was at Whipsnade, the Woburn herd numbered nearly five hundred animals. Now, the Duke felt, was the time when the animals should be distributed, because to have all the living representatives of the species congregated in one spot was risky in the extreme. An outbreak of foot-and-mouth disease, for example, could have exterminated the Père David very successfully. Therefore the Duke started by giving a pair to Whipsnade as the nucleus of a breeding herd. While I was on the Bear Section came the news that the Duke was going to let several other zoos have pairs of this deer and was going to donate yet another pair to Whipsnade. We were going to have the task of collecting the baby animals as soon as they were born at Woburn and hand-rearing them until they were of a suitable age to be transported to their new homes. The reason that this rather laborious method had been decided upon was the extreme nervousness of the deer. They would quite easily, if frightened—and they seemed more apt to be frightened by practically anything than any other animal I have met—display a stupidity that was unbelievable, such as charging a stone wall time and time again in an effort to break through. It was felt that if the baby deer were hand-reared by us they would at least be used to human beings so that perhaps unusual sights and sounds would not panic them to the same extent as if they had been caught as semi-adults.

When I discovered that I and another boy, called Bill, had been chosen to assist Phil Bates in the task of hand-rearing these deer I was overwhelmed. The babies were to be kept in two big stables, and as they had to be fed during the night as well as very early in the morning Bill and I would take it in turns to sleep in the small shed up in the woods near the stables so that we could be on hand to help Phil both at night and during the day. The great day came and we went over to Woburn in the lorry.

The parkland at Woburn was one of the most beautiful I have ever seen. This, of course, was in the days before merry-go-rounds and enormous parties of idiotic sightseers had turned the place into a sort of three-ring circus. The massive and beautifully spaced trees, the rolling greensward and the gently moving herds of deer made a picture that was unforgettable, one that would have made Edwin Landseer burst into tears of frustration.

The babies, all wide-eyed and rather startled-looking, were each inside a sack with only their heads poking out. This was a precautionary measure so that they could not stand up or try to run and break a leg while traveling in the lorry. We loaded them onto a thick layer of straw and surrounded them with bales of straw as a cushioning. Then Bill and I took up our stations in the back amongst this forest of tiny heads, and the lorry proceeded to Whipsnade at a gentle thirty miles an hour while we watched the babies closely to see what effect the journey was having on them. When the lorry first started to move, one or two of them kicked and bucked a bit inside their sacks, but they soon settled down, and by the time we reached Whipsnade several of them had fallen asleep with the bored expression of professional railway travelers.

We carried them into the stables and cut away the sacking; then, in that incredibly wobbly and pathetic manner of young deer, they all staggered inebriatedly to their feet and weaved about the stable. It was only at this point that they seemed to realize that something was missing, and so they started revolving in circles, bleating like goats—an astonishingly long, harsh "baaaa." Hastily, Bill and I milked the herd of goats that had been carefully installed against the babies' arrival, poured the still-warm, frothing milk into bottles, added the necessary vitamin drops and cod liver oil, and then, holding a bottle apiece, we entered the stable. Père David deer are just as stupid when babies as any other form of life, and at that first feed I think Bill and Phil and I got more goat's milk in our trouser turnups, in our pockets, and squirted into our eyes and ears than the babies consumed. They very soon got the hang of the idea that they should suck on the teat and thus obtain milk, but the coordination between their mouths and their brains left a lot to be desired and we had to be constantly on the alert, for they would mumble the teat around in their mouths until eventually the end was poking out of the side of the mouth, and then, scrunching it between their teeth, they would send a jet of goat's milk straight into your eye. However, within two days they had mastered this and had decided that Phil, Bill and I constituted a joint mother figure. There were eight of them and so we divided them up and put four in each stable, but as they grew bigger it became more and more difficult, for their exuberance at mealtimes was such that the moment they saw us they would deafen us with their harsh bleats and as soon as the stable door was open there would be

a cascade of deer. On several occasions both Bill and I were knocked down by the fawns and we had to roll rather quickly out of their way, for they would stamp all over us with complete lack of discrimination and their very long hoofs were exceedingly sharp.

I think it was at this time that I suddenly realized the full meaning of the term "rare." Hitherto when people talked of a rare animal I had always been under the impression that this simply meant that it was rare in museum collections or in zoological gardens, but actual rarity in numbers had not really impinged on me. This, I think, was because people tended to say an animal was rare rather as though this were an accolade, as though it were something the animal should be proud of. But with the advent of the Père David deer, and working so closely with them, it suddenly occurred to me that an astonishing number of animals were rare in quite a different sense to the way in which I had always employed the word. I started my researches on the subject and kept a massive file of the results. I did not know it at the time, but I was producing a rather shaky and amateurish version of the *Red Data Book* now published by the International Union for the Conservation of Nature. The results of my researches horrified me: figures like "total population of Indian rhinos left, 250; Sumatran rhinos, 150; Bornean rhinos, 20; world population of flightless rail, 72 pairs; Arabian oryx shot and machine-gunned to a possible total population of 30," and so on. The list, it seemed, was unending. It then that I realized what the true function of a zoological garden should be; for, while trying to protect these animals in the wild state, it was obviously of urgent necessity that breeding groups should be set up in captivity as widely spread all over the world as possible.

It was then, really, that I conceived the idea that should I ever acquire a zoo of my own, its main function in life would be this one work: to act as a reservoir and sanctuary for these harried creatures.

When it was my turn on duty with the deer I gave a lot of thought to these problems. At midnight, with the deer's great, liquid eyes glittering in the light of the storm lantern as they butted and sucked greedily at the bottles of warm milk, it seemed to me that by any standards these animals had just as much right to existence as I did. Getting up at five in the morning to give them their bottle feed was no penance. The oak woods in the first pale spears of sunlight would be as gold-green as a quetzal's tail, leaves blurred with a gossamer coating of dew, and as one walked through the great trunks toward the stable where the deer were kept the birdsong was like an enormous chorus of thanksgiving in a green cathedral. Then you would open the stable door and be knocked down by your loving charges and they would nuzzle, bleating at you, slapping you with their long, wet, warm tongues. Though the precarious state of so many animal species all over the world still filled me with despondency, at least by helping to rear Père David deer I felt I was doing something concrete, however infinitesimal the gesture was.

By far the most entrancing animals on the section were our small herd of white-tailed gnus. All the gnus are pretty unbelievable antelopes to look at, but the white-tailed has a particularly heraldic and mythical look about it. The head is blunt and the muzzle broad; the horns, curved like hunting horns, sweep down low over the eyes before curling upward into sharp points so the animal is forced to peer under them in a very myopic manner; a white beard juts out under the chin, and another tuft of bristles decorates the top of the muzzle; the white mane is thick—a forest of uncombed tufts and sprigs; and a great sporran of hair grows between the forelegs. The long, sweeping, silky white tail is their best feature, and they use it with all the elegance of an Oriental dancer with a scarf. Combined with this extraordinary appearance (which makes them look as though they have been made up out of bits of several different animals) are the gnus' extraordinary movements and the posturing they indulge in at the slightest provocation. To watch these idiotic creatures prancing, gyrating and snorting, their tails curling up over their backs, was one of the funniest sights I have seen.

Their movements were so complex that it was difficult to fit them into a category. It could really only be described as something like an acute attack of Saint Vitus' dance. Some of it resembled folk dancing of sorts, but it seemed a little vigorous. The only folk dances I have ever witnessed were danced by elderly aesthetic ladies with fringes and strings of beads, and they were nothing like the gnus' wild jitterbugging. Certainly there was a suggestion of ballet about it—of the more energetic and sweat-provoking sort—but some of the movements were too unorthodox for even the most frantically modern ballerina. This dance—or disease—is well worth watching. When the curtain rises, as it were, the gnus are facing you, bunched together, frowning through a forest of tufts and sprigs of hair. One member of the troop assumes the leadership and he or she starts the dance by giving a purring snort of astonishing loudness, a sort of preliminary "Now, girls, all together." Then the whole lot mince a few steps on slender legs; they stand again, legs quivering, tails

twitching almost in unison; then the leader gives another
snort, which invariably has the effect of making the whole
troop lose their heads. Forgotten is the grouping and precision which delights the eye in ballet. With stamping, polished
hoofs, away they go, tails curled, bucking, kicking legs
thrown out at ridiculous and completely unanatomical angles.
The leader keeps up a barrage of frantic snorts—orders which
no one obeys. Then, quite suddenly, they all stop and stare
at you from under their horns in horrified disapproval at your
unmannerly laughter.

It was, in fact, the white-tailed gnu's habit of dancing and
its insatiable curiosity that led it to the brink of extermination.
In the early days, during the colonization of South Africa,

the white-tailed gnu was found in thousands and early Dutch settlers killed it relentlessly, firstly because its meat, dried into biltong, could be used as food instead of slaughtering valuable cattle and sheep, and, secondly, because the quicker it was out of the way, they thought, the more grazing room there would be for domestic stock. So in a very short time what had been the most numerous of the African antelopes became one of the rarest. Their engaging curiosity, which would make a herd stand there peering at the hunters while they were shot down, was partially the cause of their downfall, and also the endearing fact that they loved to perform their dances and would prance and waltz round wagons bristling with guns, thus forming one of the easiest of targets. Now the white-tailed gnu is no longer a truly wild animal. Just over two thousand are left in small parks and on private farms and a scant hundred specimens in the zoos of the world.

As I watched our gnus posturing, rampant on a field of green grass, I though how dull the African scene must be now without these gay, frenetic dancers of the veld. It seems that always progress destroys the happy and original, making everything banal, replacing these joyous prancing creatures with the dull, cud-chewing, utilitarian cow.

As well as the white-tailed gnus, we had a solitary brindled gnu, an animal much the same in shape though a bit thicker-set and with a gingery fawn coat with chocolate brindles and a black mane and tail. If anything, this animal was even more mentally defective than the white-tailed gnus; his gyrations were even more wildly extravagant, and his deep, belching roars of alarm rattled from deep in his chest like machine-gun fire. He was an incredibly nervous beast and more than liable, if you frightened him, of breaking a leg or doing himself some other injury, so it was with feelings of acute apprehension that Harry and I received the news that Brinny had to be caught up and transported to London Zoo, where they had acquired a mate for him.

"That's going to be a hell of a job, isn't it, Harry?" I asked.

" 'Fraid so, boy," said Harry, stirring our breakfast of mushrooms which was sizzling in the pan.

"What are we going to put him in?" I inquired. "We haven't got anything big enough, surely?"

"No," said Harry. "They're sending a crate down on the

140

lorry Thursday. Then we crate 'im up and back 'e goes on the lorry."

It sounded very simple the way Harry put it.

Thursday dawned and the lorry arrived with a tall, narrow crate into which we had to try and cajole an exceedingly nervous, high-spirited and agile gnu. We had let Brinny out into his paddock for a brief airing that morning; I had then enticed him back into the double stable by bribing him with oats, and now we had him safely locked up in one of the loose boxes. Next we had to manhandle the massive crate off the back of the lorry and get it into position facing the door of Brinny's loose box, and then we had to raise the sliding door on the end of the crate. This took us some time and we were forced, not unnaturally, to make a fair bit of noise over it, which Brinny took grave exception to. He belched and snorted and roared and several times attempted to kick the side of the stable out.

Once having got the crate in position, we went away for half an hour to discuss strategy and to let Brinny calm down a bit.

"Now, boy," said Harry, "this is what we'll do, see. I'll be atop the crate and 'andle the slide, but once I've got that slide up I can't see when 'e goes into the crate, so you'll 'ave to tell me when to drop the slide, see? Now, I want you to take the ladder into the stable next door, then you take this bit of two-be-two, lean over the dividing wall and when 'e gets near the crate just give 'im a tap on the rump—only a tap, mind—that's all 'e'll need, just enough to make 'im run into the crate. Then, when 'e's in, you give a yell and I'll drop the slide, see?"

141

"You make it sound so simple," I said bitterly.

"Let's 'ope it is," said Harry, grinning.

We trooped back to the stable, where Brinny was still gurking fiercely, and I maneuvered the ladder into the stable next door, took my piece of wood and climbed up and peered over the partition. Brinny stared up at me, horror-stricken that I should do such a dastardly thing as to take him in the rear. His mane and beard looked wild and uncombed and gave him the air of having just arisen, disheveled, from his bed. His eyes rolled, his nostrils grew wide with every snort, and his curved black horns glinted like knives as he pranced and gyrated within the confines of the stable.

"You ready, boy?" shouted Harry from outside.

I eased my piece of wood over the partition and made sure of my foothold on the ladder.

"Okay!" I yelled. "Fire away."

Brinny, who had been staring up at me with the expression of a spinster who had at last actually found a man under her bed, naturally waltzed round to face the door and watch as the slide on the crate was slowly raised. He snorted like a volcano and minced from side to side nervously. As he was not watching me, I maneuvered my piece of wood into position. I grasped it firmly with one hand and cupped my other hand over the end. I could not have chosen a more unfortunate grasp.

"I'm going to chivvy him, Harry," I called.

"All right, boy," said Harry.

I carefully lowered my piece of wood toward Brinny's rotund and quivering backside. As the end of my stick touched his glossy hide it was as though I had touched a match to a short fuse on a barrel of TNT. Everything seemed to happen

142

at once. Feeling the stick, Brinny wasted no time; he leaped straight into the air and tried to kick his heels over his horns. He caught my piece of wood and shot it skyward like a rocket so that it crashed against the roof of the stable. My hand, which was cupped round the end of it, was therefore crushed against the ceiling as though caught by a pile driver. The pain was so excruciating that I dropped the wood and tried to struggle back over the partition, which I was half lying on. I could feel the ladder swaying under me. At that moment Brinny uttered a particularly prodigious snort, put his head down and rushed into the crate.

"Slide, Harry, slide!" I yelled desperately just as the ladder gave under me and I fell into the stable. The slide crashed into position and we had Brinny imprisoned—but only just, for he had galloped into the crate and hit the end of it with his horns, making the whole structure sway like a ship in a hurricane. Then he attacked the end of the crate with short jabs of his horns, and splintered wood started to fly in all directions. People started running about in pursuit of hammer and nails to repair the damage before Brinny could force his way out.

Harry, perched precariously on the swaying crate, peered down at me. "You all right, boy?" he inquired anxiously.

I got up a trifle shakily; my hand felt as though it had been trodden on by an elephant, and it was already beginning to swell.

"I'm okay, but I think I've bust my hand," I said.

This proved to be correct, for when I had been taken down to the hospital and X-rayed, they found that I had cracked three of the bones in the palm of my hand. I was lucky, really, not to have had them splintered and crushed through the flesh, for my hand had been sandwiched between wood and

143

wood with considerable force. I was given pain-killers—which did everything but kill pain—and told to stay off work for forty-eight hours to allow the bones to settle, as the doctor put it.

This was my first honorable wound in the course of duty, as it were, and so I was gratified that Mrs. Bailey treated me with the concern and respect for one who, if he had not actually won the Victoria Cross, had come very close to it.

That evening I was sitting by the fire nursing my aching hand when Charlie came home.

"Well, boy, you'd better get packed up," he greeted me.

"Packed up? Whatever are you talking about, Charlie?" asked Mrs. Bailey.

"Heard just now from the office," said Charlie, wiggling his slippered feet appreciatively in front of the fire. "We're to go home at the end of the week."

"Home? You mean back to London?"

"That's right," said Charlie. "You pleased, then?"

"Of course I'm pleased," said Mrs. Bailey. "But what's going to become of the boy?"

"You're to go into the Bothy. They're opening that up," said Charlie to me.

The Bothy was a huge, institutionlike building which had been constructed to house single members of the keepering staff and had never, to the best of my knowledge, been used for this purpose.

"That great barn of a place!" exclaimed Mrs. Bailey. "Why, with winter coming on he'll freeze to death."

"Oh, they've got fires and such," said Charlie.

"But what about food? Who's going to look after him?"

"Well, they said there's several people moving in," said

Charlie. "Joe from the Works staff and a new boy, and they're putting old Bill and his missis in charge to cook and suchlike."

"Never!" cried Mrs. Bailey unbelievingly. "Not that disgusting old man and his horrible wife."

Mrs. Bailey had had a long-standing feud with old Bill, a member of the Works Department, who really was a repulsive, rodentlike individual. The feud dated from the time when old Bill had delivered some firewood to the cottage and Mrs. Bailey had been complaining about her chilblains.

"You know what you wants to do for them, Ma?" said old Bill.

"No." said Mrs. Bailey, who did not like being called Ma but was always anxious to find a remedy for her chilblains. "What do you do?"

"Stick your feet in the pot first thing in the morning," old Bill advised. "A drop of pee does 'em a world of good."

Needless to say, Charlie and I had become hysterical when told this story, but Mrs. Bailey had not found it a bit funny. Now she said, "Well, I don't envy anyone being looked after by them. Here, Gerry, you better have some more pie. Eat up while you can. Gracious knows what those two will give you to eat, poor soul."

I must say I shared her view. The thought of leaving the Baileys' comfortable cottage for the great barn of the Bothy and exchanging Mrs. Bailey's lavish home cooking for goodness knows what concoction thought up by Bill and his wife was appalling, but I could do nothing about it.

CHAPTER 6

A Bumble of Bears

He licketh and sucketh his own
feet . . .
　　—BARTHOLOMEW THE ENGLISHMAN,
　　　De proprietatibus rerum

AT one end of the section a
large area of land had been thickly planted with larch trees,
and in this gloomy woodland, resembling a portion of some
North American or Russian forest, lived our pack of wolves.
There were fourteen of them, and I must say they were not
the most prepossessing animals to look at; I could quite see
how they had over the years achieved a rather evil reputation. Their pale golden eyes against their ash-gray fur seemed
slightly slanted and cunning; this impression was enhanced
by their strange gait, for they slouched rather than walked,
with their heads down and ears back. For such large and
powerful animals they moved with extraordinary grace; they
seemed to float among the shadows of the larch trees.

The wolf, I discovered, was a much maligned animal. Con-
trary to its reputation, it does not and never did spend its
entire life hunting down human beings, although, of course,
the fact that wolves on occasions have eaten men is undeni-
able. A Swiss naturalist describes with ghoulish relish how,
when the German, French and Russian troops had been

fighting bloody battles in the mountains of Switzerland in 1799, the dead were never buried but were left for the wolves to finish. Apparently the packs glutted themselves on this uniformed windfall and reputedly came to prefer human flesh to all others.

To my relief, our pack had not acquired this refinement of taste, but it was nevertheless slightly unnerving to open the gate into the Wolf Wood and push the wheelbarrow full of gory joints through the larch wood, tossing them out at intervals while the pack circled round and round you at a safe distance, snarling and yarring at each other and then rushing in in order of precedence to snap up the meat.

Wolves in the wild state mate for life and are the most devoted of parents. The average pack generally consists of the parent wolves and the youngsters of that year, so it is a family rather than a pack. However, in exceptionally hard winters several families can combine together for hunting purposes, and on these occasions the packs can be quite large. The distance covered while hunting can be enormous; one pack was accurately tracked in Alaska and in six weeks the wolves covered seven hundred miles within an area of about a hundred miles by fifty.

The wolf, of course, has always been one of the favorite animals in primitive religions as far apart as North America and Mongolia, and it fills a well-known place in witchcraft. At one time in Europe when wolves were considerably more common than they are today, lycanthropy was not only believed in but practiced. One of the most popular stories of werewolves was told by Johan Weyer, who thought it was merely a delusion brought about by prolonged torture of the

victim. The story was repeated, however, to prove the existence
of lycanthropy.

. . . Pierre Bourgot (Big Peter), Michel Verdung (or Udon),
and Philibert Mentot [were] tried in December, 1521, by the
Inquisitor General of Besançon, the Dominican friar Jean Boin
(or Bomm). Suspicion fell on these men when a traveler,
passing through the Poligny district, was attacked by a wolf;
he wounded the animal and followed its trail to a hut, where
he found the wife bathing Verdung's wounds. In his confes-
sion, Michel Verdung told how he had kept Pierre faithful
to the Devil.

Then Pierre Bourgot confessed. In 1502, a terrible storm scattered his flocks. While searching for them, he met three black
horsemen to whom he told his sorrows. One of the horsemen
(whose name was later revealed as Moyset) promised Pierre
relief and help if he would serve him as lord and master, and
Pierre agreed to bind the bargain within the week. Very soon,
he found his sheep. At the second meeting, Pierre, learning
that the kind stranger was a servant of the Devil, denied
Christianity and swore fealty by kissing the horseman's left
hand, which was black and cold as ice. After two years, Pierre
began to drift back to Christianity. At this point Michel
Verdung, another servant of the Devil, was instructed to make
Pierre toe the Devil's line. Encouraged by promises of satanic
gold, Pierre attended a sabbat, where everyone carried a green
taper burning with a blue flame. Then Verdung told him to
strip and apply a magic salve; Pierre found himself a wolf.
After two hours, Verdung applied another ointment, and Pierre
regained his human form. As a werewolf, Pierre confessed
(under torture) to various assaults. He attacked a seven-year-
old boy, but the lad screamed so that Pierre had to put on his
clothes and become a man again to avoid detection. He confessed he ate a four-year-old girl and found her flesh delicious;

he broke the neck of a nine-year-old girl and ate her. As a wolf, he mated with real wolves, and, reported Bourgot, all three men said "they had as much pleasure in the act as if they had copulated with their wives."

The three men were, of course, burned.

Quite apart from men turning themselves into wolves (and here one shares the attitude of an early disbeliever in witchcraft who said that he had silenced many witches by saying, "If you can turn a woman into a cat, can you now turn a cat into a woman?"), the wolf itself has had any number of magical powers attributed to it. T. H. White, in his delightful translation of a twelfth-century bestiary, quotes Ulysses Aldrovandi:

Rhasis was being frivolous when he reported concerning wolves' hair: "If the eyebrows are anointed with the same, mixed with rose-water, the anointed one will be adored by the beholder." And really I think it even more ridiculous and merry when it is said that backward men and women can be brought to lust by the tie of a wolf's pizzle (dried in an oven). This is like the statement about a wolf-skin pouch, which, if worn with a dove's heart tied up inside it, saves one from falling into the snares of Venus. Rather of the same sort is the story of Rhasis, who cites ten disciples of Democritus, people who certainly escaped safely from the enemy by carrying the scrotum of a wolf on their lances. In the same way, Sextus tells us about the Traveller who made his journey safely by carrying with him the end bit of a wolf's tail. Also, according to Vuecherius, if one hangs up the brush or the pelt or the head of a wolf over the stall, the beasts will not eat unless it is taken away. With the same tail, so Albertus Magnus says, if it is tied above the mangers of sheep and cattle, the wolf itself can be frightened off: and that is why people bury them in farms, to keep these brutes away.

152

With all this remarkable publicity, it is scarcely to be wondered at that the wolf in fact can hardly match up to the popular conception of him.

Our female wolves came into estrus once a year and generally gave birth to their young in May. During the time the females were in season there was, of course, an immense amount of fighting amongst the dogs in the pack. Although these fights sounded and looked savage, with much clopping of jaws and baring of teeth, accompanied by yarring snarls and whines, they never appeared to actually draw blood. When the time drew near for the bitch to have her cubs, she and the dominant dog will excavate a complicated burrow under the roots of a larch. Here she would give birth to her cubs, generally three or five in number. When we went in with the wheelbarrow to feed, we had to be cautious and avoid these nurseries; otherwise, the female would get panicky and start carrying her cubs all over the wood in an endeavor to guard them against us. As soon as the cubs were old enough to be weaned, both parents would regurgitate semidigested meat for the young—a sort of wolf equivalent to tinned baby food.

On moonlit nights, especially if there was a touch of frost in the air, our wolves would hold great operatic parties. The wood would be silver-striped with moonlight and you could just see the black outline of the animals as they flitted from one patch of shadow to the next; then, suddenly, they would all merge together and, throwing back their heads, would utter their wild and plaintive howls that, in amongst the tree trunks, had a sort of echoing quality, as though they were singing in a cave. Their eyes would glint where the moonlight caught them, and their throats would swell as they got more and more excited and threw themselves with ever greater enthusiasm

into the song. Watching them like this, you were very tempted to believe all the things that have ever been written about wolves.

Wolf song is one of the most beautiful animal noises, so I was not altogether surprised to discover that wolves apparently share my mixed feelings regarding the bagpipes. In 1624, when wolves were a commonplace in England and Ireland, Sir Thomas Fairfax related the story of a soldier in Ireland who got his passport to go to England:

> . . . as he passed through the wood with his knapsack upon his back, being weary, he sat down under a tree, where he opened his knapsack, and fell to some victuals he had; but on a sudden he was surprized with two or three wolves, who coming towards him, he threw them scraps of bread and cheese, till all was gone; then the wolves making a nearer approach to him he knew not what shift to make, but by taking a pair of bagpipes which he had, and as soone as he began to

play upon them, the wolves ran all away as if they had been
scared out of their wits: whereupon the soldier said, A pox
take you all, if I had known you had loved music so well, you
should have had it before dinner.

Those wolves must have been pretty hungry to devour
bread and cheese; our wolves were extremely particular and
dainty about their food.

I remember one day when a little old lady watched me with
bated breath as I wheeled my barrow with its gory load
through the Wolf Wood, tossing out the joints. As I came out
of the wood and locked the gate behind me, she approached
me.

"Excuse me, young man," she said, "but what sort of meat
is that?"

I was feeling in a particularly facetious mood and so putting
on my best poker face, I replied, "Keepers, madam. It's an
economy measure. When the keepers get too old to work we
feed them to the wolves."

Just for a slight second a look of incredulous horror spread
over her face before she realized she was having her leg
pulled.

But on a moonlight night, lying safely curled up in bed,
you could listen to the flutelike cries of the wolves and it
gave the night a certain magical charm.

Compared to the wolves, the bears we looked after were a
very mixed lot. They looked as though their ancestry combined European, Asiatic and North American species in a sort
of potpourri. The largest was the male, who had been christened—in that flash of genius that overcomes quite ordinary
people when naming animals—Teddy, and he was a great,

rolling, gingerbread-colored fool, with the tiny, rather frantic pleading eyes of a village idiot, a large, pink, retroussé nose, and exceptionally long, curved, tortoiseshell-colored claws which he spent a lot of time manicuring by sucking them. Teddy had a shambling, rather pansy walk that made his claws click together like castanets when he moved and caused amused consternation among the public.

" 'Ere, Bill, 'ere's a bear tap-dancing."

"Don't be silly, mate, 'e's a clockwork bear. That's a motor wot you can 'ear. 'Spect the keeper winds 'im up every morning."

It was I who discovered what should have been obvious from his ponderous walk, from his portly form, and from the habit he had of sitting on his hind legs with one paw on his heart: that Teddy was really an operatic tenor in disguise. I was cycling past the bears' enclosure one day when I heard the most extraordinary noise—a cross between the high-pitched buzzing of a mosquito, with deeper overtones, and an occasional falsetto squeak like the expiring cry of a fairy soprano. Puzzled as to what could possibly be producing this strange and unbearlike noise, I got off my bicycle and investigated. There, sitting on his ample ginger bottom behind a blackberry bush, was Teddy, one paw clasped across his chest and the claws of his other paw stuffed into his mouth, singing to himself. It seemed incredible that such a massive beast—he must have weighed all of three hundred and fifty pounds—should produce such an oddly feminine sound. His tiny boot-button eyes were half closed, and he swayed slightly as he sang. I watched him for a while and then I called to him. He opened his eyes with a start, removed his claws from his mouth, and gazed at me in what looked very like embarrassment. I called him over to the bars and gave him some black-berries I had found. He sat in front of me like a great ginger Buddha, taking the glittering black fruit from my hand very delicately with his prehensile lips. When he had finished I took a deep breath, arranged my vocal chords to cope as well as possible with the imitation and gave Teddy a chorus from "White Horse Inn."

He looked at me, startled, for a moment and then, to my delight, he laid one fat paw across his chest, stuck the claws of the other into his mouth, closed his eyes and joined me in song. It was an inspired rendering, and we were both, I think,

sorry when lack of breath—on my part—brought it to a halt. After this I frequently used to have musical half hours with Teddy, and when I was cleaning up paper and other debris inside the barrier rail the monotony of the task was greatly relieved by Teddy, who would follow me round singing lustily. One day we were leaning against the bars gazing into each other's eyes and getting some pretty good harmonization on "You May Not Be an Angel" when I happened to glance round and there were three nuns standing riveted on the path watching us. As I looked they gathered their robes about them and moved on; not by a flicker of an eye did they give the impression that they had been witnessing anything unusual, but the situation greatly embarrassed Teddy and me.

Teddy was a bear of such charm that I was almost inclined to believe the story of the lady-killing bear that I found in Topsell.

> Phillipus Coffeus of Constance, did most confidently tell me, that in the Mountains of Savoy, a Bear carryed a young maid into his den by violence, where in venereous manner he had the carnal use of her body, and while he kept her in his den, he daily went forth and brought her home the best Apples and other fruits he could get, presenting them unto her for her meat in very amorous sort; but always when he went to forrage, he rouled a huge great stone upon the mouth of his den, that the Virgin should not escape away: at length her parents with long search, found their little Daughter in the Bear's den, who delivered her from that savage and beastual captivity.

It is curious that the so-called hairy Ainus, a primitive people who are found on the Japanese island of Hokkaido, tend to revere the bear and have a very similar type of story.

The legend, however, is of a woman who had a son by a bear, and apparently many of the Ainus who live in the mountains pride themselves on being descended from a bear. They are called Descendants of the Bear and they say of themselves, "As for me, I am a child of the God of the Mountains. I am descended from the divine one who rules in the mountains." However, the fact that they consider the bear a sacred animal is a somewhat mixed blessing as far as the bear is concerned, for they have every year a Bear Festival.

A bear cub is captured and brought to the village, and if it is very tiny it is suckled by one of the village women or fed by hand or mouth to mouth. As it grows it plays about in the hut with the children and is treated with great affection as a pet, but as it grows a bit too big for this treatment it is shut up in a wooden cage, where it stays for two or three years, being fattened up, as it were. Then, in September or October, the festival takes place.

The villagers begin by apologizing to their gods, saying they have kept the bear as long as they possibly could with their meager resources, but now they are forced to kill him. If the village is a small one the entire community takes part in the festival. When everybody is assembled in front of the cage the village orator speaks to the bear and tells it it is about to be sent to its ancestors. He asks its pardon and hopes that it won't be angry with them. Oddly in contradiction to this propitiation, the bear is then tied up with ropes and let out of the cage, and showers of blunt arrows are fired into it to infuriate it. When it has exhausted itself struggling to get free from the ropes, it is tied up to a stake, gagged and then strangled, its neck being placed between two poles which are pressed together, everyone in the village showing great eagerness in helping with this operation. Then an arrow is shot into the bear's heart, but very carefully so as not to shed any blood. The men sometimes drink the warm blood of the bear in order to gain the courage and other virtues that the animal posesses, and they smear it on themselves in order to ensure success in hunting. When the bear is dead it is skinned, its head is cut off and set up in the east window of the house with a piece of its own body, a cup of its own meat boiled, some millet dumplings and dried fish. Prayers are then addressed to the dead animal and, amongst other things, it is asked to be broad-minded enough to go to its mother and father and then return to the world so it can be caught all over again and reared for sacrifice. It has been noticed that at the beginning of the festival the woman who has reared the bear weeps copiously, but she nevertheless joins in with the strangling with great alacrity and soon recovers her *joie de vivre* once the bear is dead, which is a rather fine commentary on human nature.

I was lucky enough to be still working on this section when Teddy's two wives had babies. Harry knew that they were pregnant, but the exact date they were due to give birth was guesswork. Then we saw them collecting leaves for their dens and we knew that the births must be imminent. The dens, which were scattered among the bramble bushes that filled the enclosure, were beehivelike rondvals of stone covered with earth and turf. The females squatted down a few yards from their respective dens and with curved arms started to drag all the leaves and the grass in the vicinity toward themselves, cherishing the bundles against their fat bellies. When the supply of bedding gave out in one spot they retreated backwards, shuffling on their behinds, and started on a new patch of grass. When they had collected almost more than they could hold, they backed carefully into the dens to deposit their loads. The nests thus constructed were about a foot or eighteen inches deep and some five feet across. After this nest-making, some time elapsed, and then one day Harry and I were passing the bear enclosure and Harry suddenly stopped and cocked his head on one side.

" 'Ear that, boy?" he said.

I listened and heard a high-pitched noise emanating from one of the dens—the sort of squeak a rubber toy would make.

"They've 'ad 'em," said Harry with satisfaction.

To celebrate, I went down to the pub on the village green and bought two bottles of beer to drink with our elevenses. I was very excited by the whole event, and I asked Harry over our celebratory pint when we could see the cubs.

" 'Ave to wait till their eyes open, boy," he said.

"When's that?" I asked eagerly, whipping out my notebook to record the vital fact.

"Three weeks or thereabouts," said Harry. "Three weeks and then we can go in an' see 'em and sex 'em."

I could hardly wait. If I had known what was in store for me I would not have been so eager. But at last the great day dawned.

"We'll go in with them bears today," said Harry casually that morning.

Naturally I thought he meant the babies.

"To sex the cubs?" I asked.

"Right, boy," said Harry. "There's a photographer chap coming down from one of the London newspapers about ten-thirty, so you get a couple of ladders down there and lock Teddy up in one trap and the females up in the other. Understand, boy?"

"Yes," I said. Mine not to reason why, though I longed to know what we were to do with two ladders.

I managed to get Teddy into one trap with the aid of some blackberries and a chorus from "On the Isle of Capri." His wives were more suspicious and reluctant, but eventually they succumbed to their greed when bribed with fat, sticky dates.

Eventually Harry's diminutive figure appeared with a tall, gangling photographer in tow and Denis, a keeper from another section.

"Everything right, boy? You got 'em separated like I said?" asked Harry.

"Everything under control," I replied.

Harry checked on the locks of the traps and then rubbed his hands together briskly.

"Now, boy," he said, "get them ladders over the side."

I must explain at this point that the bear enclosure, which covered about an acre of land, was bounded on three sides by a twelve-foot iron-barred fence with a pointed overhang. On the fourth side the earth had been banked up and cemented so that here you went up some steps and then looked down on the bears some twelve feet below you. It also gave you a panoramic view over the whole enclosure. It was at this point that Harry wanted the ladders put down. I was still puzzled as to why we needed two ladders, but I dutifully lowered them over the side and made sure they were secure.

"Right, boy, come on," said Harry, and he vaulted over the rail and scuttled down one ladder as rapidly as a cockroach, and I followed him.

The female bears, seeing us inside the enclosure and walking toward the dens, started roaring unpleasantly—a sort of snarling moan that told us in no uncertain terms what they would do to us if they could get out. When we got to the first den Harry got down on all fours and crawled inside. There was a moment's silence and then he crawled out again awkwardly, dragging with him two yarring, reluctant little animals that took my breath away. To my astonished eyes they looked like two electric-blue teddybears from some toy shop. On closer inspection of the infants, however, I saw that their fur was not electric blue but was certainly a sort of Persian-cat blue. Their claws, like their father's, were very long, sharp, and a pale-amber color, and their circular eyes were bright China blue. With all these fairy-tale qualities to commend them you would have thought that they would have the most charming and diffident of characters; but no, they yarred and snarled shrilly; they slashed at us with their long claws, as anchorlike as blackberry thorns, and snapped at us with fragile, needle-sharp white teeth.

" 'Ere, boy," said Harry, holding up these two enchanting but lethal bundles, "get 'old of these and I'll get the other two."

He shoved them unceremoniously into my arms, and it was rather like trying to embrace a couple of muscular fur coats full of fishhooks. Eventually, when Harry had extracted two more of these babies from the other den we made our way back to the ladders. I had never realized until then (such are the limitations of a sheltered life) how difficult it is to climb a ladder while carrying two malevolently inclined bear cubs. Both Harry and I arrived at the top scratched, bitten bloody, but more or less unbowed. Here we stood trying to look debonair while the cubs were photographed from every angle. I discovered then—and I have had no reason since to change my view—that photographers are a callous and insensitive species. A demand to "get his head round a little so we can get a profile" may seem a simple enough request to them but may mean the loss of a couple of fingers to you.

Eventually, the photographer finished—at least I thought he had. But then he turned to Harry and said, "How about that shot of the mothers with them?"

"Oh, that's all fixed," said Harry. "We'll do it now."

I remember thinking that Harry was being a bit overconfident, for once the cubs were released I knew they would make a beeline for the shelter of the bramble bushes and once they were ensconced in there photography would be impossible.

"Down you go, boy," said Harry, "and don't let those cubs go until I tell you."

After a balancing act that would have won me applause in any circus, I got down into the enclosure again and placed the

164

cubs thankfully on the ground, retaining a firm grip on the scruff of their necks. Harry joined me with his two squirming babies and plonked them down alongside mine.

"Now, boy," said Harry, "this is what we do, see? We'll 'old the cubs 'ere while Denis lets the females out of the traps."

I stared at him in disbelief, holding my cacophonous twin cubs in an iron grip. He was not joking—he meant it.

"Harry," I said, "you're *nuts*. When those bloody bears get out with these cubs yelling, they'll—they'll . . ."

My voice died away, paralyzed at the thought of what they would do, but Harry was not listening.

"Denis," he yelled, "you ready?"

"Yus," came Denis' voice faintly from the direction of the traps.

"Harry—" I began frantically.

"Now, boy," said Harry soothingly, "you 'old them cubs till I tell you to let them go, see? Them bears won't touch us once they get the cubs."

"But Harry—" I started again.

"It's quite all right, boy. We've got two ladders, see? When I says let go, you let go and nip up your ladder. Nothing to it," said Harry. "Now you ready, boy?"

"But, Harry—"

"All right, Denis, let 'em out," yelled Harry.

The next few moments were crowded.

To say that I thought Harry and I were behaving like lunatics is putting it mildly. A she-bear robbed of her whelps—in this case *two* she-bears—God! Even Shakespeare would have had more sense. At that moment the two females in the traps stopped their roaring noise; there was the clanging sound I knew so well—the sound of the sliding doors on the trap being raised. Then came an ominous silence. We could not see the traps because of the bramble bushes.

"Any moment now, boy," said Harry cheerfully.

"Harry—" I tried once again.

"Ah!" said Harry with satisfaction, "Here they come."

I had never realized until that moment that two determined and muscular bears could walk through a complicated, twelve-year-old bramble thicket as though it were tissue paper. It made the same rather fragile tearing noise, too. And, then at a distance of about twenty feet, Harry and I and the four bear cubs were face to face with the irate mothers. The babies, seeing their parents, started wriggling madly and squealing greetings at the top of their lungs. The mothers paused, orientating themselves, gave a couple of outraged sniffs worthy of Stevenson's rocket, and then charged us, growling in a raucous manner. They did not run toward us; they bounced, like two great, hairy balls, and somehow this method of approach added menace to the whole thing. Their turn of speed was amazing and they loomed larger and larger. They got to about twelve feet away and I began to think that all was lost.

"Righto, boy. Let 'em go," said Harry, and he released his two cubs.

Never have I let go of an animal with such speed and thankfulness. In fact, in my enthusiasm I almost flung the cubs at their mothers. Then I made for the ladder behind me and skimmed up it with simianlike speed and skill. At the top I paused and looked back. Sure enough, as Harry had predicted, the two bears had come to a halt when they got to the cubs and were too intent on licking and fussing them to worry about us. We pulled the ladders up and I wiped the sweat from my face.

"Harry," I said firmly as we made our way back to the zebra sheds, "I wouldn't do that again for a thousand quid."

"Well, you did it for two pounds ten," said Harry chuckling.

"What d'you mean, I did it for two pounds ten?"

"That's what the photographer tipped me," said Harry. "A fiver. You can have 'alf of it, boy."

It did enable me to take my current girl friend out to the cinema, but I still did not think it was worth it.

CHAPTER 7

A Loom
of Giraffe

---

*A very gentle beast, and of a good
conscience.*
—SHAKESPEARE, *A Midsummer Night's
Dream*

JUST after the Baileys had, to my infinite regret, left and I had moved into the stark, reformatorylike atmosphere of the Bothy, I was also put on a new section. This was known as the Giraffe Section. It was presided over by one Bert Rogers, a quiet, kindly man with a face like a cherry, wind-polished, and chicory-blue eyes. In spite of his somewhat shy and retiring nature he answered all my endless questions about the animals with great patience and humor, and he was immensely proud of the animals in his charge.

The centerpoint of the section was, rather unfortunately, in the middle of Bluebell Wood. This wood, so charming in spring, left a lot to be desired at this time of the year, the beginning of winter. It was surrounded by large areas of grassland, and so the wind whipped across it at us bitingly. The name Bluebell Wood was, at the time I joined the section, a euphemism. It conjured up a picture of green oaks with the misty smoke of a million flowers about their roots. Instead of which, the great tree trunks shone with rain, and a bright-green mold spread like a stain upon them. It was now a dismal, dripping wood where the wallabies squatted in disgrunted groups and the muntjaks stole by humbly, diminutive in the cathedral of great trunks.

It was, of course, Peter the Beringo giraffe who loomed over the rest of the section in every sense of the word. He occupied the largest, best-designed and most handsome animal house in Whipsnade. It was built out of wood in the shape of a half moon, and the interior had a beautiful parqueted floor. Attached to this, of course, was a large paddock, but, owing to the vagaries of the English climate at all times of the year but in the early winter months in particular, Peter spent most of his waking hours pacing up and down the length of his ballroomlike establishment.

The first morning I joined the section, Bert, having explained our multifarious activities to me, said, "Now, lad, first job we've got to do is to clean out Peter."

"Do you, er, go in with him?" I inquired cautiously.

" 'Course," said Bert, faintly surprised.

"He's, um, tame, then?" I said, liking to get things straight in my mind, with the episode of the bears still fresh in my memory.

"Who? Old Peter?" said Bert. "He wouldn't hurt a fly."

And, so saying, he handed me a brush, opened the door and ushered me into the echoing Albert Hall-like structure which was Peter's home.

Peter's mate had died long before I came to the park, and without her Peter had become fretful and gone off his food. In order to give him the companionship he obviously missed, a kid of curious color and doubtful ancestry had been introduced into his house. By the time I joined the section this kid—

inevitably christened Billy—had grown into a large and rather ugly goat but with a considerable personality and charm. When we went into Peter's house that first morning Peter stood in the far corner, a wisp of hay hanging from his mouth, his jaws moving rhythmically, and a faraway look in his eyes. He resembled nothing so much as a Regency buck trying to make up his mind which cravat he would wear that morning. Billy, acting as he always did, as a sort of cross between a public-relations officer and a social secretary for the giraffe, uttered a welcoming bleat and came bustling forward to investigate me and see whether either I or any of my wearing apparel was by any remote chance edible.

"You just take it nice and easy, lad," said Bert. "just go on sweeping up gentle like. Don't make any sudden movements. He doesn't like sudden movements—they frighten him, then he might kick. He'll probably come up and say hello presently."

Looking at the towering spotted form at the other end of the house, I had no particular desire to get on a more intimate footing with him.

"Well, I'll go and feed them buffalo," said Bert.

"What? Aren't you staying?" I asked, startled.

"No," said Bert, "doesn't take two of us to sweep out this place. 'Spect you'll have it done in a jiffy."

I will, I thought, if I'm not kicked to death in the process.

So Bert left me incarcerated in the house, with Peter musing at one end and Billy endeavoring to extract one of my shoelaces and consume it. Bert had given me no time limit for cleaning of the house, and the parquet flooring made it an easy surface to sweep, so I thought I would devote a few minutes to making my mark with Billy and just let Peter get used to

the idea of a stranger in his midst. I found some lumps of
sugar in my pocket and with the aid of these put my friendship with Billy on a firm footing. He fell upon them with
such enthusiasm you would have thought he had never had
a square meal in his life, yet his Shetland-pony-sized body
with its curious gingery-yellow fur was exceedingly well
covered. It was while I was feeding Billy sugar lumps that
Peter decided to move. He swallowed the last bit of hay and
then came pacing down the length of the house toward me. It
was really rather eerie; one got the same sense of unreality
one would get—the same shock—if one suddenly saw a tree
uproot itself and drift across the landscape. For Peter did
drift. The mechanism that controlled those vast limbs was
incredible, for here was the tallest mammal on earth coming
toward me and yet he moved as casually and as gracefully as a
deer and as silently as a cloud. He was not ungainly; he was
completely unhurried, and his beauty of movement did not
allow you to notice his disproportionate limbs or his great
height. Giraffes are, after all, built for clumsiness, but there
was no ugliness here. He came to a stop some twelve feet
away from me, by which time his head was directly above me,
and then slowly lowered his head and peered into my face.
The length and thickness of his eyelashes had to be seen to be
believed, as did the liquid beauty of his enormous dark eyes
gazing at me with a spirit of gentle inquiry. He sniffed at me
with the utmost delicacy and politeness. Then, having apparently decided that I was harmless, he turned and sauntered
off. His tail was a long, sweeping pendulum of ivory silk
hair and he swished it gently from side to side; his complicated pattern of honey-brown and cream was a unique and

beautiful mosaic. From that moment on, Peter and, indeed, every giraffe that ever lived had me under its spell.

As I worked on the section I was fascinated to watch the relationship that had grown up between Peter and Billy. That Peter had a tremendous affection for this unattractive beast was quite obvious, and that the goat cared about as much for Peter as he did for anything else in this world was quite obvious. Billy had an all-consuming—if I may use the phrase—hobby, and that was his perpetual search for anything that was remotely edible. Peter would gaze down at his friend's squat, pinky, straw-colored body with limpid eyes, nuzzle him with utmost gentleness and affection, and step over him with great care. Billy, on the other hand, should he wish to get to a spot and find that Peter was in the way, had much more forthright tactics. He would simply put his head down and butt one of the great spotted legs until Peter, with an air of nervous apology, stepped out of the way. Billy had humorous yellow eyes, a short, dapper beard and a very ungainly, almost square body about the size of a Shetland pony. There could have been no greater contrast between the two animals; Peter looked every inch the aristocrat, the well-mannered dandy, whereas Billy was quite obviously nothing but a common, voracious goat with a Past, but he had all the humor and unflincing audacity of his breed to carry him through life, combined with an ability to make the best of things. There was absolutely no doubt who was boss in Peter's house. I am sure that if placed in the same quarters with a rhino Billy would have had it at his mercy inside twenty-four hours.

He would, once he got to know me better, occasionally take a few minutes off from his life's work of trying to eat something that was not edible and would then honor me with a game. His idea of a game was curious and strenuous. It consisted quite simply of putting his head down and charging me. My side of the play consisted of trying to stop the full force of his attack in my cupped hands, at the same time stepping to one side. This required considerable patience and practice, and should I not be up to form I would find myself lying on my back, painfully winded, while Billy stood over me shaking his beard in my face, his yellow eyes full of malicious laughter. If I spent too long in regaining my feet I would quite possibly find half my tie missing, for sport of any kind always increased Billy's appetite tremendously.

To watch Peter feeding was quite an education. His enormously long, bright-blue tongue would raise itself round a sprig of hay with incredible delicacy. You got the impression indeed that the tongue almost had a life of its own, for it could choose and reject food with unerring accuracy while Peter appeared to be in a trance. To see him pick up food from the floor was another extraordinary sight. For this he employed two methods. The first was to bend both front legs at the knee until his head was low enough to get at the food. The other was more frequently employed and was a more complicated and dangerous method. He would edge his huge front legs apart, spreading them wider and wider, inch by inch, until he could swing his long neck down and pick up the delicacy with his tongue. He employed extreme caution with this maneuver, for should his foothold give way he would go crashing down, legs spread out, and both his shoulder blades, his legs and most possibly his back would be broken.

Even when you knew that Peter had accepted you, cleaning his house was inclined to be an eerie experience. Sweeping vigorously with the brush, I would not hear his almost inaudible approach, the faint scuff of his padded hoofs on the parquet, and the first warning would be his deep and contemplative sigh down the back of my neck. I would then look over my shoulder and see him towering some twenty feet above me, and the surprise of this was not calculated to soothe the nerves. His great dewy eyes would be full of curiosity, his underjaw would move rhythmically from side to side as he chewed the cud, his nostrils would widen, and he would breathe another gust of hay-scented breath at me. Then his great neck would swing his head some sixteen feet away, and with his slouching stride he would drift off to probe with his blue tongue in the hayrack. Peter was never vicious while I worked with him, but I knew that a well-aimed kick from one of those giant hoofs could kill a lion should the need arise, and so I treated him with caution. The main thing was not to scare him. This, of course, applies to any animal that you are looking after, but the giraffe is of an extraordinarily nervous disposition and if frightened might well staff off into a hysterical canter that it is almost impossible to stop and which could end in either heart failure from exhaustion or possibly a broken leg. This, of course, would be an extreme case; normally, if frightened, the automatic impulse is to lash out with the hind legs or bring the head sweeping down in a scythelike motion which literally cuts the enemy down like grass.

In a zoo, of course, the immense size of a giraffe and his beautiful skin, like a vivid tapestry, make him seem to be one of the most noticeable of animals, whereas in fact in his natural state he is probably one of the best camouflaged. Gordon Cumming, writing about the giraffe, states that

> in the case of the giraffe, which is invariably met with among venerable forests, where innumerable blasted and weather-beaten trunks and stems occur, I have repeatedly been in doubt as to the presence of a troop, until I had recourse to my telescope, and on referring to my savage attendants I have known even their practised eyes deceived, at one time mistaking these dilapidated trunks for camelopards and again confounding real camelopards with these aged veterans of the forest.

Peter's silence was very noticeable and was accentuated, I think, by Billy's habit of talking to himself in a series of muttered "baas" while he pottered to and fro looking for food. I think Peter's silence was more noticeable because it was more complete—not only vocal but physical. His large hoofs whispered on the wooden flooring, and the sudden whistling swish of his tail was always startling. He would stand there quite still, looking straight through you, contemplating some obscure and absorbing memory; delicately, almost absent-mindedly his blue tongue would appear, curve gracefully round a sprig of hay and pull it into his mouth; he would chew automatically, his expression unchanged, still with that faraway look in his eyes. Tall, slender, with his long sensitive face, his melting eyes, that long-legged swinging walk, he was a perfect Beau Brummel. He could really, I decided, be described only by one word—he looked cultured.

The only time Peter ever did anything which could be remotely described as vulgar was when he chewed the cud. He would stand contemplating me as I swept the floor of his house, his underjaw moving rhythmically from side to side; then he would swallow the mouthful and his jaw would become still, a glazed expression would spread over his face, and if you looked you would think that his mind was full of beautiful, poetical thoughts. He would have an air of waiting for something, At last it would come and it was so incongruous that it was almost laughable. Deep in the poet's stomach you could hear a curious rumbling which ended in a sort of pop. A ball of food would make its appearance at the base of his long neck and, bulging the skin as it went, would travel upward with all the majesty of a department-store lift. The ball was generally about the size of a coconut, and it would end its travels by rolling into his mouth. A satisfied expression would replace the look of thoughtful genius, and Peter's lower jaw would recommence its monotonous movement. I could never make out whether he could control the supply of food. If he could not, I fear it must be embarrassing in the wild state to have, say, one's declaration of love suddenly interrupted by this loud and stately regurgitation of one's breakfast.

It was not until I was working with Billy and Peter and so had them together for comparison that the giraffe's curious mode of locomotion really impinged on me. The first day I was on the section I was watching the two animals and Billy, on one of his gastronomic quests, walked across the floor of the house closely followed by Peter. Watching them, I felt there was something queer, that their movements did not seem to match. Then I saw what it was. While Billy walked in a normal mammalian way—that is to say, the right front foot forward, followed by the left hind foot—Peter moved both right feet together. This gave him that curious long-legged walk with that immense, swinging, lopsided stride. It also accounted for the curious way that giraffes sway when cantering. Both right legs being off the ground at the same time, the full weight of the body is thrown onto the left legs and so the head and the neck are swung over to the right to counteract; when the left legs come into play the neck is swung over again. So they go dipping and swaying across the grass, their necks swinging from side to side like huge checkered pendulums.

The fact that Peter was incarcerated with Billy caused, I am afraid, considerable confusion in the minds of the great

British public. Most of the visitors leaped to an inaccurate conclusion after one hasty glance.

"Ooh, look! A baby—a baby giraffe! Ooh, isn't he *sweet!*" they would cry. To which, in most cases, Billy would reply with a hearty and completely ungiraffelike "baaa." This, however, would have no effect on his audience.

"Wonder why he hasn't got any spots like his mum," they would ask each other.

"Perhaps they come after, like."

"Wonder why he hasn't got a long neck?"

"Well, he's only a baby, see. It's got to grow."

Peter would gaze at them reprovingly from a distance, displaying none of the maternal instincts that were expected of him. Billy would be far too busy pressing up to the wire begging them for tidbits to worry about what people thought he was.

Billy had worked the process of soliciting food down to a fine art. I have seen him, five minutes after disposing of three large turnips, rush frantically out to meet a visitor, with a rolling eye and an unsteady gait that argued a normal diet only a shade above starvation level.

"He seems to be awfully hungry," the victim would remark to you, giving you a look that implied volumes.

"Oh, he's always hungry," you would reply with a gay laugh. "He eats anything. Here, Billy, try this." And you would offer Billy a fir cone.

At any other time he would fall upon the cone as though it were his favorite food, but not now. He would give it a quick glance and turn away.

"Is that *all* you give him to eat?" the visitor would ask.

"Oh, Lord, no," you would protest. "Why, he gets an excellent diet—exactly the same as the giraffe."

And at that moment Billy, who would be groveling in his food pan, would reappear with a small piece of cloth hanging from his mouth, which he would chew rhythmically, wearing an expression of extreme martyrdom. I discovered that you simply could not win with a goat.

If Peter was a gentle aristocrat, the same, I am afraid, could not be said of his nearest neighbors on the section, our herd of African buffaloes. They looked and in fact were the direct opposite to Peter. Their dusky witches' blackness gave them a faintly macabre appearance as they moved in a dark and glowering line across the green of their paddock. The five cows were led by a massive old bull, and he was a magnificent though rather frightening beast. The great gnarled trunk of his horns hung low over his tiny red-rimmed eyes, and his tattered ears would turn toward you with a fierce interrogativeness as you passed his paddock. Owing to his habit of

rolling in his shed before it was cleaned out, his flanks were encrusted with dried dung which had cracked without falling off, making him look as though he were wearing a uniform brown jigsaw puzzle. The herd had the typically thick, sweet smell of domestic cattle, but it was remarkably strong and was even apparent at some distance in the open paddock.

One thing I could praise the buffaloes for was their conduct as a herd, for they moved with an almost military precision. The other herds of animals in the park were, on the whole, an unruly lot; when moving together they would fight and push in a solid and ill-mannered wedge for the best positions. Not so the buffaloes; to see them crossing the paddock for a drink was to see a perfect example of orderly progress. In single file they would approach the pool, the old bull leading, followed by the rest in the order of their seniority. There was no unladylike or ungentlemanly shoving or pushing, none of that deplorable get-out-of-the-way-or-I'll-give-you-a-jab-in-the-behind attitude of the bison. When they reached the pool they would spread out and drink deeply and unhurriedly and then stand knee-high in the water, musing, as still as an intricate jet carving.

The old bull, I soon discovered, had a temper as black as his hide, and he would have periodic fits where his efforts to kill someone—anyone—were frightening while they lasted. At other times he was comparatively tame and he would stand with his pink-rimmed eyes half closed while you scratched his head and ears. His great patent-leather nose was always shining moistly and he had the disgusting habit of blowing great clouds of frothy spittle out of his mouth and nostrils. If you were not careful when you scratched him he would suddenly heave a great sigh of contentment and the front of your coat would be white with bursting bubbles that he had blown onto you. At other times the devil would get into him and you had to measure the distance you stood from the wire, for he was swift and deadly.

Along one side of the paddock ran one of the main paths, and down this I would cycle each evening on my way home. Should the bull be in one of his bubble-blowing moods I could traverse this hundred yards without so much as an ear being twitched in my direction; but should he be in his evil mood he would swerve away from the main herd and, with his swift, lumbering gallop, would thunder along the fence at my side, tossing his giant horns and producing a deep chesty roar which was not the most attractive sound I have ever heard. From a distance this portly canter did not impress one as being very fast, but I have traveled along that path at a dangerous speed on my bicycle and the bull kept pace with me effortlessly, rattling his horns along the wire, roaring with open mouth, his hoofs spreading wide with each thrust of his thick, stubby legs, leaving black scars on the brightness of the turf. The old bull had no name, so I christened him Ghengis, feeling that he could, if he put his mind to it, do as much damage as any Tatar horde.

On the days when he was particularly misanthropic he had a very curious rite that he would indulge in. He would lower his massive head and then, with a certain effort, place one foot carefully in the arch of his horn; then he would stand there ducking his head up and down, almost overbalancing himself, or else he would perform a sort of waltz, going round and round on three legs, pretending that his hoof was too intricately caught up to be released. These performances generally lasted about half an hour. Why he did this was not

at all clear; certainly none of the cows attempted to emulate him. Indeed, they seemed vaguely embarrassed by their leader's childishness and would remove themselves to the farthest corner of the paddock while this was going on. I could only presume that he put on this performance for the same reason that a lion paces up and down its cage or a polar bear or an elephant will weave from side to side—a soothing and interesting habit to pass the time till the next meal. Ghengis appeared to go about it with a feeling of deep interest in the outcome: Would he succeed in unraveling his hoof from his horn? See next week's thrilling installment.

One of the old bull's harem was a cow with only one horn, and not long after I joined the section she gave birth. The baby looked not unlike an ordinary domestic calf, except for his disproportionately large ears. He was an attractive shade of chocolate brown, with great bulbous leg joints and a delightfully uncontrollable tail. But two days after he was born we noticed that although he was trotting round the paddock with his mother he did not seem as strong as he should be. Bert and I stood and watched him.

"What d'you think's wrong with him, Bert?" I asked.

"I dunno," said Bert, "but he's not right, that I *am* sure of."

At that moment, to our complete surprise, we saw the baby endeavoring to graze. Now it was obvious that there was something very wrong, for a two-day-old calf does not start grazing if he is getting his proper food. With the aid of oats and hay we managed to entice the cow to the fence, and we discovered that her udders were quite dry. The baby, finding no milk where it should, had, in desperation, started to imitate its mother in an effort to find food.

"What are we going to do?" I asked Bert.

"Well, there's only one thing *to* do," said Bert. "We'll have to get the youngster out and feed him on the bottle."

To remove the calf of a doting buffalo cow from under her nose is not the sort of thing one has to do or, indeed, wants to do every day. After a considerable amount of trouble we succeeded in separating the cow and the calf from the rest of the herd and locked them up in their shed. At that moment, inevitably, Billy Beale arrived, the bush telegraph having informed him that something was afoot. He explained encouragingly that he had come along to see me gored, or, if not me, somebody else.

We had now arrived at the interesting part of the whole affair: we had to go into the shed and take the calf away from the cow.

186

"Now," said Bert, explaining my role to me, "I'll go in and drive the cow into one corner. You grab the calf and hoik him out, get it?"

"Yes," I said.

All the stories I had read about the fearsomeness of African buffaloes floated through my mind at that moment. Bert armed himself with a long and extremely fragile-looking stick; then he entered the shed, and, with a fair display of trembling nonchalance, I followed him. The cow was standing at the far end of the shed, with the calf under her nose. She looked about five times as big as she normally looked in the paddock. As we entered, her ears spread out and she uttered a surprised and somewhat peeved snort.

"Now," said Bert, "I'll keep her occupied with this stick here and you rush in and grab the calf. All right?"

I admitted that the idea seemed sound in theory and wiped the palms of my hands on my coat. Without further ado Bert swept forward, saying, "Come on, now, my girl, come on," in a very authoritative tone of voice. It took the cow so much by surprise that, to my amazement, Bert actually managed to drive her into the corner of the shed opposite to the calf.

"Now!" he shouted suddenly, and, uttering a brief prayer, I rushed forward, wrapped my arms round the calf's body, tried to lift him, and found to my horror that he was far too heavy. He snuffled at me in a friendly sort of manner and trod heavily on my instep. Finding I could not lift him, I changed my tactics and, grasping him firmly by the front legs, endeavored to pull him along. The calf suddenly woke up to the fact that I was attempting to remove him from his mother, and the idea did not appeal to him in the slightest.

187

As I pulled, he dug his stubby feet into the floor and became as immovable as a rock.

"Bert!" I called desperately. "I can't shift him."

Bert glanced rapidly over his shoulder, and at the same moment the cow decided that she had been intimidated for quite long enough. The next few seconds were full of activity, with both Bert and me making desperate attempts to get on her hornless side. We eventually retreated, more or less unscathed, to the door, where, after some argument, I enlisted the help of Billy to help me drag the calf. Once again Bert went in with his stick and for the second time he managed to drive the cow off, and Billy and I rushed in and grabbed the reluctant baby. We got off to a bad start, for I trod on Billy's foot by mistake and was then tripped up by the calf barging against my legs, so we both fell down full length in what must have been the bull buffalo's favorite wallow. It was certainly succulent enough to be. Finally we got to our feet, grabbed the calf and hustled it out of the shed. We were sweating profusely and covered from head to foot in dung. Then we wrapped the kicking, struggling, bleating infant in sacks and he was placed in the zoo van and rushed off to that part of the park where baby animals were kept and reared. Both Billy and I had to go home for a bath and a complete change of clothing before we were civilized company again.

Now that winter was approaching I was beginning to feel even more depressed living in the Bothy. If one sat downstairs in the huge living room one was forced to take part in inane conversations with the other inmates. The only alternative was one's bedroom, a cell-like place, cold enough to ship beef in. My wages did not allow me on these long winter evenings to go to the pub, and so on most nights I was wrapped up in bed by seven, reading or writing up my notes. So, not unnaturally, I looked forward to Thursday evenings (when I had dinner with the Beales) with the sort of yearning that a Buddhist has for Nirvana. The warmth and brightness of the Beales' living room, the happy conversations about animals, riotous card games with the captain inventing his own rules, songs round the piano, and the gorgeous conflagrations of the captain's curries—all this was wonderful to me, who was, as far as I was concerned, incarcerated in something closely approaching a Siberian detention camp.

Periodically, too, there would be incredible journeys into Dunstable or Luton to see a film that had taken the captain's fancy. Billy would search me out in the park: "Daddy says to come early tonight—we're going to the cinema." So I would arrive early and the captain would be waiting impatiently in the hall looking three times life size in his huge overcoat, a gigantic muffler round his neck, his narrow-brimmed trilby pulled down on his forehead.

"Ah, Durrell," he would bark, his spectacles glittering feverishly, "come in, come in. At least *you're* on time. Can't understand what these women *do*. What's your mother doing, Billy?"

"Dressing," Billy would say succinctly.

The captain would lumber up and down, muttering and consulting his watch.

"Gladys!" he would bellow at last, no longer able to contain himself. "Gladys! Where the hell are you? *Gladys!*"

Distantly, from the bedroom, would come Mrs. Beale's voice uttering some soothing excuse.

"Well, hurry up!" the captain would roar. "D'you know

what time it is? Gladys! . . . *Gladys!* I said do you know what time it is? If you don't hurry up we'll miss the beginning of the film. Gladys! . . . I'm not shouting—I'm just trying to hurry you bloody women up. . . . I'm *not* swearing. I just want you to *hurry up!*"

Eventually Mrs. Beale and the three girls would appear, twittering, and the captain would usher them outside and into the car like an enormous sheepdog, grumbling to himself. He would wedge himself behind the wheel, Laura and Mrs. Beale beside him, and the rest of us would jam ourselves into the back. After a series of terrifying roars from the engine and a series of strangled grinding noises from the gears we would lurch forward.

"Ha!" the captain would say with satisfaction. "Soon be there now."

This was in the days when petrol was still rationed, a fact that annoyed the captain, who treated all forms of rationing as examples of the Government's implacable hatred of himself and his family. So in order to save petrol he had evolved a system which was as novel as it was useless. When the car reached the top of a slope the captain would switch off the engine.

"Push!" he would roar. "All together, *push.*"

The first time I heard him give this remarkable order I thought that we had run out of petrol and that the captain wanted us to vacate the car and push it from behind. Nothing could have been further from the truth. What the captain meant by "push" was that you all lurched to and fro in your seats. By this method, he assured us, you gave the car extra momentum as it cruised down the hill.

"*Push!* Come on, *push*," he would bellow, throwing his great bulk to and fro. "Push, Gladys!"

"I *am* pushing, William," Mrs. Beale would gasp, red-faced, throwing herself backward and forward with all the abandonment of a puppet in a Punch and Judy show.

"Well, you're not pushing enough! You all, behind, come on, *push*. Harder! Harder!"

"I can't push any harder, William," Mrs. Beale would gasp, "and I don't think it makes any difference."

"Of *course* it makes a difference," the captain would snarl. "It makes *all* the bloody difference if you do it properly. Come on, push harder—*harder!*"

The car would reach the bottom of the hill and start up the opposite slope.

"All together. All together. Harder—*harder!*" the captain would roar frantically, and the car would be full of gasps and grunts as we all flung ourselves about like a Rugby scrum.

Eventually, the car would creep to a halt; the captain would apply the brake.

"Look at *that*," he would rasp irritably, pointing a spade-shaped hand out the window. "We've only got to that gorse bush. Last time we got as far as that may tree. I told you, you aren't *pushing* properly."

"But we can't push more than we have pushed, William."

"Rhythm. That's what you lack," the captain would explain.

"But we can't be expected to have rhythm when we're pushing, dear."

"Of course you can," the captain would roar. "Any bloody wog knows that. Rhythm, timing. You're not doing it *properly*. Now let's try it again."

"I shall be so glad when petrol rationing is over," Mrs. Beale would confide to me in a whisper.

"Well, it's not my fault, is it?" the captain would shout truculently. "It's not *my* fault the bloody Government only gives a teaspoonful of petrol. I'm only trying to *eke it out*."

"Yes, dear. Don't swear. And I didn't say it was your fault."

"It's *not* my bloody fault. I'm trying to help and you're not doing it properly."

"Very well, dear. We'll try again."

The car would reach the crest of the next hill and start downward. The captain would switch off the engine once again.

"Now," he would shout, "take your timing from me. Put your backs into it. All together—one, two, three, *push*. One, two, three, *push*. You're not pushing, Gladys! You're *out of step!* How can you expect to get results when you're out of bloody step? One, two three, *push*. Gladys, concentrate!"

So, jerking and gasping, we would creep on our way. However dull the film was, our trips to and from the cinema were anything but dull.

CHAPTER 8

A Superiority of Camels

———— ◆ ————

But the Commissariat cam-u-el, when all is said an' done,
'E's a devil an' a ostrich an' a orphan-child in one.
   —KIPLING, *Oonts*

WINTER came upon us like the sudden opening of a tomb. Almost overnight it seemed that the last multicolored banners of autumn leaves had been wrenched from the trees by the wind and built up in great moldering piles that smelled like plum cake when you kicked them. Then came the early-morning frost that turned the long grass white and crisp as biscuit, made your breath hang in pale cobwebs in front of you and nipped at your fingertips with the viciousness of a slamming door. Then came the snow, in great flakes like Madeira lace, settling in a smooth milk-white coating over the countryside, a layer up to your knees and drifts seven feet deep, a covering that muffled all sound except its own squeaking and rustling voice as you walked on it. Now the wind whipped unrestricted across at you like a saber-cut, squeezing the tears from your eyes, freezing the melting snow on the trees and guttering into fluted icicles like a million melting candles.

I had been moved from my love affair with the giraffe and was now on the section known as "The Camels." On this section the main animals were the herd of Bactrian camels, a herd of yaks, a pair of tapirs, and sundry antelopes and deer. The section boss was a Mr. Cole ("I'm Mr. Cole to you, young fellow-me-lad," he had said to me the first morning), who bore a remarkable physical resemblance to the camels in his charge. His sidekick was old Tom, who was a delight—a huge shire horse of a man who shambled round painfully on feet so encrusted with bunions that his shoes looked as though they were full of potatoes; his tiny, kindly eyes were the clear, hot blue of a jay's wing; and his swooping eagle nose, through the careful application over the years of beer and homemade wine, had assumed the bright redness and shiny patina of a holly berry. Old Tom had never married, but he kept in close and affectionate touch with all of his fifteen children. So kindly a man was he that his face was set in a permanent smile, and his wheezy voice was so full of affection that even if he simply said "Good morning" you felt he was saying it to you because he loved you more than anyone else in the world. In consequence, everyone adored him and would go out of their way to do things for him as he shambled, beaming, round the zoo, looking like Falstaff's grandfather.

The main herd of camels, consisting of six females, was led and ruled by Big Bill, a huge animal with overstuffed humps like a French armchair, great plus-fours of curls on his legs, and an expression of such sneering superiority that you longed for him to trip over something and fall down. He would stand towering over you, his belly rumbling, squeaking his long, greeny-yellow teeth together and staring at you with a disbelieving disgust as though you were a child murderer or something similarly obscene. Apart from this positively Victorian belief in his superiority he was an untrustworthy

beast and would not hesitate to lash out at you with one of his great pincushionlike feet if he felt that you were not giving him the respect that was his due. As you were never quite sure what Big Bill considered to be an affront to his dignity, life with him was hazardous.

Once, on my way to feed the tapirs, I decided to take a shortcut by climbing the fence and crossing the camel paddock. Big Bill was standing in the middle of the paddock ruminating, and as I got near him I greeted him.

"What ho, Bill old boy!" I said jovially.

It was obvious that my familiar attitude did not appeal to such a superior animal. Big Bill's jaws stopped moving, and his pale yellow eyes fastened on me. Then he suddenly stepped

forward very swiftly, his head lunged down with open mouth, and he sank his long, discolored teeth into the clothing on my chest, lifted me off my feet, shook me and dropped me. Mercifully, I was wearing a thick tweed coat and a very thick rolltop pullover, so that his teeth sank into this instead of the wall of my chest. As I lay on the ground he wheeled round and lashed out with his hind leg. Desperately I rolled to one side, and his great hoof missed my head by inches. I got to my feet and fled. It was the last time I took a shortcut across Big Bill's paddock.

The most elderly of Bill's wives was a sedate matron known

as Old Gran, and while I was on the section she gave birth.
The baby must have been born early one morning, for when
we arrived at eight o'clock we found him lying in the straw
under his mother's bulging stomach, looking utterly bewildered and dejected, his fur plastered down and wet from Old
Gran's greeting wash. As she was the most docile of the herd,
I could examine the infant without risk of being kicked in the
face. He was extremely thin and bony, and his long legs were
too rubbery to support him to begin with. On his back, hanging forlornly down one side, were two triangular patches of
skin. These miserable objects would later swell and fill out

until they became his humps. Old Gran seemed extremely proud of him and she nuzzled him the whole time to make sure that he was quite safe down there below her, and then she would put her head back and stare at the roof of the stable with an expression of ineffable smugness.

After twenty-four hours the baby could walk, or, to be more accurate, he could, after considerable effort, hoist himself onto his legs. After this preliminary effort the whole performance began to lack reality. He had not as yet obtained full control of his lanky legs with their great, bulbous joints. In fact, at times it seemed as though some other power were in control of these necessary adjuncts and that he was trying manfully to get possession of them. He would stagger a few steps, his knees buckling under him, and the more they bent the more worried became his expression. Then he would come to a stop, swaying violently, and consider the problem. But the longer he stood still the less inclined his legs became to support him. His knees would fold up, his body would lunge wildly from side to side, and then, quite suddenly, the whole scaffolding of his limbs would cave in and he would fall heavily to the ground, his legs sticking out at such weird angles that it was only their elasticity that prevented them from being snapped. Grimly determined, he would climb upright again by painful stages and then set off at a brisk run, but even this method was no use. His legs would shoot out in the most unpredictable directions and he would stagger wildly. The faster he went, the more involved became the antics of his legs. He would leap in the air in an effort to disentangle them from each other, but the knot would be too intricate and once again he would fall in a heap on the ground. But he persisted in these exercises every morning, while nearby his mother would stand chewing the cud and watching him proudly.

After two days he had at last succeeded in controlling his legs to a certain degree, which was really quite an achievement. He was so proud of his accomplishment that he took daring risks such as gamboling like a lamb, which sometimes ended disastrously. This gamboling was as laughable as his first attempts to walk. He would frisk around his mother, bucking and bouncing, his hump flaps waving like pocket handkerchiefs out of a train window. Sometimes his legs would let him down and he would fall heavily to the ground. This would have a sobering effect, and when he got to his feet he would walk behind his mother very sedately. Then his feelings would get the better of him and he would be off again. The rest of the herd considered him a nuisance, for he was not a very good judge of distance and would frequently bump into one of them, tripping them up and causing a hiatus in their orderly progression. Quite frequently he would receive a kick from an outraged matron whose rear he had assaulted by tripping over his own feet while executing a particularly complicated and beautiful gambol.

In a separate small paddock, with their own shed, housed there as a temporary measure, lived three of old Bill's sons. They were about two years old and had been separated from the main herd in case old Bill took exception to their presence. They were without doubt three of the most idiotic and irritating animals I have had to cope with. They stood about six feet high and their humps were still fairly wobbly with youth and they had a certain amount of difficulty in controlling their gangling legs. Their paddock was small and so it had been stripped bare of grass by their great fat feet, and it was this dust bowl one had to sweep up every morning with the three young camels' assistance.

When you arrived they would be clustered round the gate staring into each other's faces benignly and forming such a solid phalanx that you could not get the gate open. Eventually, after much pushing with brushes and spades, they would become dimly aware of the fact that you wanted to come in and that they were in the way, so they would move and stand peering at you with a vacuous expression of deep interest as you entered the paddock. As you walked across it they would follow you, breathing affectionately down your neck, treading on your heels and occasionally missing their footing so that they barged into you and you fell over. No amount of threats or cajolery could make them stand in one spot while you swept up; they would follow you around, and wherever you decided to brush, there one of the camels would be, standing beaming at you. With an enormous amount of labor and a torrent of blasphemy you would have to hurl yourself against the animal and push its reluctant body over six feet so that you could get on with the sweeping-up process. By the time you had moved one camel from the spot you wanted to sweep, one of the others would have taken up his position on the same ground. The whole process of sweeping their paddock was frustrating in the extreme, but at last it would be swept and garnished, and heaving a sigh of relief, you would let yourself out and lock the gate behind you. The three young camels, standing in the center of the paddock, would stare after you misty-eyed, as though watching the departure of their dearest friend. Then, each wagging its tail in a ridiculously lamblike gesture, they would produce three identical steaming piles of ordure in the middle of the area you had so carefully cleaned.

That camels have readily adapted themselves to a harsh life is borne out by what Lydekker says of them:

> The Bactrian camel feeds chiefly upon the saline and bitter plants of the steppes which are rejected by almost all other animals; and displays a curious partiality for salt, drinking freely at the brackish water and salt lakes, which are so common throughout its habitat. Instead of confining itself to a strictly vegetable diet, the Bactrian camel, according to the reports of Prejevalski, will, when pressed by hunger, readily devour almost anything that it may come across, including felt blankets, bones and skins of animals, flesh and fish.

Although I never saw Big Bill eat anything other than oats, mangolds and hay, he adored the great blocks of rock salt we gave the camels and would break great pieces off in his yellow teeth and scrunch them up like a crackle of musketry while gazing at you witheringly.

Two of my favorite animals on the section were a pair of South American tapirs who had been christened with the most unlikely names of Arthur and Ethel. Tapirs look rather like a cross between an elephant and a horse, with a touch of pig thrown in for good measure. They look, in fact, very like the reconstruction of some of the prehistoric horses except for their little rubbery trunks. Rotund, benign, with little, twinkling eyes, they waddled round their paddock like Tweedledum and Tweedledee.

Once a day, Tom and I would sit down with a great pile of potatoes, carrots, turnips and mangolds in front of us and carefully chop them up into small pieces, which we would put in a sack. Then Tom would haul himself to his bunioned feet, hoist the sack onto his back and lumber off to feed the tapirs. The tapirs would greet his appearance with cries of joy, a curious piping noise like somebody rubbing a wet thumb over a balloon, a strangely birdlike noise for such stolid animals. To see old Tom, with his swooping eagle nose, his bowlegs and his shambling gait, moving round the paddock with the tapirs in hot pursuit always used to amuse me, for if Mr. Cole looked like the camels which were his pride and joy, old Tom looked like nothing more or less than a red-faced tapir.

In the forests of South America the tapir appears to have only three enemies: man, the great snakes and the jaguar. Lydekker says:

> . . . they are much sought after by the native South-American hunters for the sake of their flesh and hide. The flesh is said to be juicy and well-flavoured, and both in appearance and taste resembles beef. The skin, which is of great thickness and strength, is cut into long thongs, which, after being rounded and treated with fat, are used for reins and bridles. It is, however, unsuited for shoe-leather, as it becomes very hard and unyielding when dry, and very soft and spongy when wetted. The hairs, hoofs, and certain other parts are used by the natives as medicine; the hoofs being sometimes hung round the neck as charms, and in other cases ground to powder and taken internally. . . .
>
> Next to man, the worst foes of the tapir are the larger cats; the jaguar preying largely on the American species, and the tiger attacking its Malayan cousin. It is said that when an American tapir is attacked by a jaguar, it immediately rushes into the thickest cover in the hope of dislodging its assailant, which from the thickness of the animal's hide is unable to

obtain a firm hold on its back. It is further reported that the tapir is not unfrequently successful; and, in any case, many of these animals are killed with the marks of jaguar's claws on their backs.

Although our tapirs never displayed any signs of bad temper, after I had learned that they could in moments of stress knock you down, trample on you with their sharp hoofs, and rips bits off you with their great teeth, I treated them with a certain amount of circumspection and gave up slapping their behinds with quite such exuberant familiarity when I went into the paddock with them.

The other creatures on the section were our great herd of yaks, and these were rather charming animals. The yak is a very curious member of the ox family, both in shape, with his very high shoulders sloping down to his tail, and in the fact that the bulk of his fur grows underneath. If you look at a yak you will see that its legs, its belly and the lower part of its tail are covered by a thick shawl of fur, while the fur on its back and neck is comparatively short. The pure wild yak is black or a very dark chocolate, and we had some of these, though the majority of our herd was spotted with white, cream, ash gray and black, a sign of their long domestication.

What the camel is to the deserts, the yak is to the high places of the world. Yaks have very limited intelligence but enormous stubborn tenacity, rather like professional soldiers, and their great strength and determination will get them to the most extraordinary places over terrain that could not be covered by any other animal. They appear to be utterly impervious to cold and, in Tibet, choose partly frozen muddy pot-

holes by the edge of icy torrents as their wallows. The paddock in which we kept our herd had a large pond in it, and now that winter was upon us it was necessary to go twice a day and break the ice on this. It was one of the first and most unpleasant jobs in the morning. The reason for this was that if the ice grew too thick the baby yaks would venture out on to it, to be followed by the adults; the combined weights would probably break the ice and the yaks would fall in and drown. When we went to perform this duty the yaks would come galloping over the snow to greet us, bounding curvaceously, swishing their tails like stock whips and occasionally, in a fit of exuberance, standing on their heads and kicking their heels in the air. The breath would squirt out of their nostrils in great white plumes of steam, and the snow would squeak, rustle and whisper musically under their hoofs.

You would spear a bale of hay on the tines of your pitchfork, haul it up onto your back with a quick wriggle and twist, like an expert wrestler throwing an opponent, and then march steadily through the field, up to your knees in snow, while the yaks surrounded you in a great furry, sweet-smelling avalanche of goodwill, rubbing themselves up against you and occasionally trying to steal a mouthful of hay from the bale on your back; the resulting tug would, if you were not careful, pull you flat on your back. When you got near the pond you would remove the wires from the bale and scatter the hay in bunches over the snow, and the great beasts would gather round it, munching mouthfuls with tremendous satisfaction.

As you approached the edge of the pond with your spade, all the baby yaks would follow you, gamboling round you like enormous puppies. As you broke the rim of ice round the pond into a jigsaw of shattering ice pieces, the baby yaks would plunge their muzzles in and drink thirstily. Then they would get down into the water and roll, splintering and scrunching the ice under their bodies. If you were not quick enough in beating a retreat at this point, you would find that half a dozen baby yaks would get to their feet and shake themselves simultaneously, with the result that you would be drenched to the skin with icy water.

It was curious that although the yaks were almost as big as the North American buffaloes and certainly as potentially lethal, one never got the feeling that they were ill-disposed, and I took risks with them that I would never have done with any of the other large ungulates in the park. The babies loved to be played with, and when the snow was deep and soft I would launch myself at a passing baby and grab hold of his great plumelike tail. The animal would rush off at top speed, and if you clung on and relaxed he would drag you across the surface of the snow like a sledge. Eventually you would let go, and immediately the yak would stop and look round at you in astonishment that you should so easily give up such an excellent game.

After you had mucked out their shed and done the other chores, your hands would be scarlet and blue and frozen stiff; then was the time to approach one of the larger yaks as it fed placidly and plunge your hands into the thick fur over its ribs, where the warmth was like that of a furnace.

General Kinloch, writing in the 1800s of the yaks in Tibet, observes:

> Yak seem to wander about a good deal. In summer the cows are generally to be found in herds varying in numbers from ten to one hundred; while the old bulls are for the most part solitary or in small parties of three or four. They feed at night and early in the morning, and usually betake themselves to some steep and barren hillside during the day, lying sometimes for hours in the same spot. Old bulls in particular seem to rejoice in choosing a commanding situation for their resting-place and their tracks may be found on the tops of the steepest hills, above the highest traces of vegetation. The yak is not apparently a very sharp-sighted beast, but its sense of smell is extremely keen, and this is the chief danger to guard against in stalking it. In the high valleys of Tibet where so many glens intersect one another, and where the temperature is continually changing, the wind is equally variable. It will sometimes shift to every point of the compass in the course of a few minutes, and the best-planned stalk may be utterly spoiled.

The fact that winter, with its attendant miseries, was now with us did nothing to improve my feelings about having to live in the Bothy. The trouble was that when I arrived and took up residence with the Baileys I had been spoiled; I doubt whether anybody had been as cosseted as I was on my first job away from home. The Baileys had given me a tremendous warmth and affection and had accepted me as a son, but in the nicest and most unrestricted sort of way. Charlie would encourage me to show off by telling him long stories of my family and my brief past life. He would laugh, probably not believing, and then repeat the salient points to himself silently, beaming quietly. Meanwhile, Mrs. Bailey would guide me on the sterner things of life.

"Have another helping. . . . Are your shoes clean? . . . Is she a *nice* girl? . . . Don't stay out too late. Remember, your mother wouldn't like it. . . . Have another helping. . . . No, if you want to drink don't go to the pub, dear. Bring it over here, it's more comfy. But no more than two pints, mind."

Those lovely bickerings over me:

"Leave the boy alone, dear. Why shouldn't he have a pint?"

"It's not the pint I mind, Charlie, as well you know, but if he starts going over *there*, well, what would his mother say?"

"His mother'd say he wants a pint."

"If he brings it back here it's much more comfy and we all know where we are. But not more than two pints, dear, it's almost time for bed."

Now all this was gone and the drabness of my life in the Bothy had to be experienced to be believed.

With the white mist pressing like a huge muffling paw over the countryside, I would be glad to see the blurred nimbus of orange light that seemed to pulse in the shifting veils. With face and hands aching with cold, one was glad of any shelter, even such as was offered by the Bothy.

The hall would be only a degree warmer than outside and

by peering in the dim light at the row of pegs arranged in a rack along the walls I could ascertain who was in and who was not. Some evenings I was first; Joe's battered mackintosh was absent, together with his greasy cap, Bill's thick, dusty blanket coat and Roy's nondescript piece of clothing which might once have been a good Burberry.

Whether it was a good thing to arrive first for tea was rather a moot point. There were only two ways: arrive first and have to sit making inane conversation with Mrs. Mansfield or arrive late and eat half-cold food and drink lukewarm tea with an ill-disguised expression of disgust. I generally braved the former, but even then there were snags.

A blast of heat would greet me in the kitchen where we had our meals. Mrs. Mansfield would be preparing our tea, and the strong smell would tell me that it was fish again. Resigning myself to my fate, I would sit down at the table. Mrs. Mansfield, who among numerous other physical disabilities included the somewhat doubtful attribute of acute deafness, would be oblivious to my arrival and would continue cutting and buttering bread.

She was a short, ugly little woman with a curious malformation of the jaw, which gave her Cockney speech a slushy and sometimes incomprehensible overtone. Her eyes were small and dark, and she screwed them up in an unprepossessing manner which argued defective eyesight. Her hair was an extraordinary forest of tufts and tails, never tidy, for the simple reason that it was not thick or long enough to be managed successfully, so it hung limply round her head. I had realized, fatalistically, that it was only a matter of time before I found a portion of it in my food.

I would sit there trying not to pay any attention to her method of preparing the food, but it had a macabre fascination. On the table would lie a loaf of bread. She would pick it up and hold it against her dirty apron so that she could cut a slice. The slice thus produced was grasped in one grimy paw while with the other she slapped the butter on and smoothed it over the surface. During this process some of the butter would attach itself to her thumb. She would suck it off noisily and then grasp the bread again, wrapping her saliva-covered thumb around it affectionately as she continued with the job. Having counted the slices lying on the cloth, she would proceed to the larder for a plate to put them on. Returning, she would notice me for the first time. A bright smile would distort her features.

"You back?" she would inquire.

I would smile and nod.

"You back?" she would repeat, twisting her head on one side, as if listening.

This time I would not reply, as it was unnecessary. She continuously repeated herself.

She would wipe the dust off the plate with a gaily colored towel hanging behind the door. At least it had been at one time gaily colored, but as it had hung there for a fortnight and had been used continuously for dishes and hands, some of its finer points were obscured. The bread would be piled onto the plate and she would shuffle over to the stove, talking squelchily over her shoulder to me.

"Tea won't be long. I've been to Luton. I've been out—out to Luton. Only just got in. Only been in five minutes."

"Have you?" I would inquire disinterestedly, watching

while she removed the lid from the saucepan and released a cloud of steam heavily laden with fishy odors. She would sniff into the bubbling interior, resembling more than anything one of Macbeth's witches.

"Fish," she would point out brightly, replacing the lid. "Do you like it?"

As we had had fish for tea for the last two or three months, it was difficult to reply to this question.

The rattle of the door handle would herald the approach of someone who could take my attention from her food preparation. Joe. He would stand in the doorway smiling gently, his lean, handsome face red with cold and the fine hairs on his cheekbones gleaming like copper in the light.

"Good evening, Joseph," I would salute him.

"Good evening." He would smile and advance into the kitchen, his large boots scrunching and squeaking on the tiles. He would sit down heavily and survey the table.

"Christ! Fish again," he would state rather than ask.

"Yes," I would answer glumly, stirring the remains on my plate with the fork. "We'll be growing tails soon."

Joe would give one of his wheezy, subterranean chuckles.

Mrs. Mansfield would place the haddock before Joe, smiling at him.

"Fish," she would explain, pointing.

"Aye," Joe would reply, "I can see that."

"You're home early," she would prattle on. "Been working hard?"

"Aye," Joe would shout, his eyes gleaming amusedly, and then to me in a lower tone, "I haven't done a damn bloody thing all day. Too bloody cold."

We would chew in silence for a few moments. Then Joe would wash down a mouthful of haddock with tea and belch gently.

"Where's t'boy?"

"Roy? He's not in yet. Neither's Bill."

"Bill's working too hard to come back for his tay," Joe would observe, and give a husky laugh.

Presently, Roy would appear, a pale, quiet, shy youth who was incapable of raising his voice sufficiently for Mrs. Mansfield to understand him easily. He would sit down and smile nervously at Joe and me. Mealtime was a source of considerable embarrassment to him. Mrs. Mansfield he could not talk to; Joe he was frightened of; and so he would turn to me, sensing in some way my sympathy for his embarrassment.

"Ooh!" Mrs. Mansfield would exclaim, having just perceived him. "You in?"

Roy would give a perfunctory nod and gaze at the table. For the third time Mrs. Mansfield would inform us that the food we were enjoying was fish. In particular, she would inform Roy, who would receive the news with complete expressionlessness. We would all sit silently, with the exception of the lady, who would champ and suck her food noisily.

The fog would press damply on the windows. Monotonously the clock would tick on the dresser, the kettle would snore gently on the fire, and above this cacophonous symphony one could hear the steady squelch, squelch, squelch of Mrs. Mansfield's dentures tearing and squeezing the fish into a pulp. She would pause occasionally to gulp noisily at her tea.

"Bill's late," she would observe. "Working on the pump, he is."

"Aye," Joe would say, then add as an aside, "That's why we've got no bloody water."

Roy would giggle nervously. Mrs. Mansfield would smile uncomprehendingly.

"They do have their little joke, eh?" she would say to me archly.

"Rather," I would bellow.

A noise in the hall, and the master of the Bothy, Bill himself, would appear. He was perhaps the most interesting and repulsive member of our community, a shuffling, humorless, round-shouldered individual with flat, close-set eyes, set with cunningness in his lined and ratlike face. He always smelled stale. I have never met anybody who was so consistently right about everything; Bill knew best and would tell you so with all the arrogance of the truly ignorant.

"Ah," he would say by way of greeting, shambling to his seat.

"Evening, Bill," Joe would say, his eyes twinkling maliciously. "Been working overtime?"

"No," Bill would say. "Them buggers lost the screws. I told 'em not to touch them. Would they listen? Ho no."

Bill always had a clear globule of liquid suspended from his long nose. I would watch fascinated while it quivered and trembled with his movements, clinging with precarious tenacity to its hairy perch. Its owner would survey the plate placed before him.

"Haddock," he would say, with pride in his discovery.

"Fish," his wife would correct. "You like a bit of fish, don't you?"

"Yus," Bill would say and slice it delicately.

His movements were careful and so slow as to be almost

214

reptilian. He would shovel the food into his mouth and munch it with that supreme indifference that you see in a cud-chewing cow. His cheeks would bulge and roll like two bolsters with the movement of his jaws. He would breathe heavily through his nose.

Joe would lean back and light his pipe, sending thick wreaths of chest-constricting smoke across the table. Roy would be still struggling with his haddock. Mrs. Mansfield would be lost in some tiny thought that had percolated into her numb brain.

"You going out tonight?" Bill would ask me.

"No."

I always spoke monosyllabically to Bill, as it helped to still the flood of dull reminiscences which lurked continuously behind his most casual utterance, awaiting only the right cue to be brought forth for everyone's boredom.

"Ho," he would ruminate, "so you'll be in, then, eh?"

Bill's logic was good but rudimentary. He liked to make sure of his points.

I would nod.

"Whassamatter?" he would inquire, "don't she love you no more?"

"Oh yes, but she's going out with somebody else's husband," I would joke.

They would all laugh, including Mrs. Mansfield, who would not have heard but would not want to be left out.

The inevitable would now happen. Bill's globule would give up the unequal contest with the laws of gravity and drop accurately onto the forkful of haddock which was traveling toward his mouth. He would chew it methodically.

"Well," Joe would say, "*I'm* going out."

He would get up and clump off, whistling through the echoing hall. I would feel Bill's ratlike gaze turn on me and, to avoid the endless and tedious commentary on his day's work, I would follow Joe's example. As I reached the hall I would hear Mrs. Mansfield asking Roy if he liked fish.

CHAPTER 9

Odd-Beast Boy

———◆———

*All that is comprehended of flesh and
of spirit of life and so of body and soul
is called animal—a beast—whether it
be airy as fowls that fly, or watery as
fish that swim, or earthy as beasts that
go on the ground and in fields, as men
and beasts, wild and tame, or other that
creep and glide on the ground.*
—BARTHOLOMEW THE ENGLISHMAN,
De proprietatibus rerum

FOR a happy two or three months I became what I could only describe as "odd-beast boy"; that is to say that I had a tiny section of my own, which consisted of half a dozen pairs of huskies and two pairs of arctic foxes to look after, but as these did not fill my time I was sent to various sections to take the place of anyone who was on a day off. This was fascinating, as it allowed me to renew my acquaintance with a number of the animals that I had got to know, like Paul the tiger; and as I moved on to a new section every day virtually, the work was never lacking in interest.

I had never had to deal with huskies before, and the first day I treated them with a certain amount of circumspection, for they were massive animals, but I soon discovered that although they were willing at the drop of a bone to fight each other to the death, they exhibited toward all members of the human race an almost embarrassingly exuberant bonhomie. The largest of the group was an immense cream-colored bitch called Squash. I did not appreciate the aptness of this name

until the first time I went into her paddock. Beaming goodwill, her panting tongue looking as long and as red as the average VIP carpet, she hurled herself at me in an endeavor to lick every portion of my face in order to show her undying devotion to the human race. Standing on her hind legs she came to slightly over six feet, and so to have this immense white powderpuff suddenly hurl itself at you and rear up onto your shoulders sent you, not unnaturally, reeling back against the wire, whereupon Squash would live up to her name and unless you were pretty nimble you were liable to collect a couple of broken ribs. Once the first mighty embrace was over, however, she would behave slightly more sensibly but would nevertheless still persist in walking round and round you as you swept out her paddock, wagging her tail vigorously and uttering moaning love calls at you. Occasionally she would hit you across the shin with her tail, and it was rather like being kicked by a horse. In spite of the fact that one had to be in as good training as, if not slightly better than, the average all-in wrestler for working with Squash, she was a beautiful and most endearing animal. All the other members of the husky pack were attractive and lovable enough in their way, but it was the great, waddling Squash who really had the personality.

Phil had told me when I had taken over the huskies that Squash had been mated and would in due course produce puppies, so I kept a careful eye on her and gave her all the best tidbits of the meat, and, reverting to the poaching I had indulged in when on the Lion Section, I searched the local farmers' hedges for eggs to give her. It was exceedingly difficult to keep a daily check on Squash so that one would know when she was about to have pups, because, first of all, any advance on your part was treated with such wild excitement that the whole thing would get out of control, and she wore such a massive coat of fur that it was extremely difficult to judge her girth to see whether her teats were full of milk without undertaking a prolonged wrestling match so that you could dig your fingers sufficiently far into her coat to be able to judge the signs. Gradually, as time passed, her teats grew heavy with milk, and then one morning she greeted me with less than her normal exuberance and, after a quick lick, disappeared to her hutch, where I could hear the whewling cries of the pups. She sat outside the hutch wearing an expression that could only be described as smug, and when I peered into the bed of straw I saw six fat babies rolling about uttering high-pitched squeals and blundering into each other like a group of drunks outside a pub. Four of them were ash gray and white in patches and two of them were the same creamy white as their mother. They were fine, healthy babies with a thick layer of fat, tight, shiny coats, and blunt, nuzzling heads like a strange type of otter.

Although it was not Squash's first litter, from the pride she displayed in them you would have thought it was. As soon as I entered her paddock to sweep out in the mornings, having licked me good day and sent me reeling against the wire she would rush to her hutch, pick up one of her puppies and bring it to me. If I crouched down she would place the puppy in my lap and stand there breathing stertorously, her tongue flopping out, wagging her tail, while I fondled the puppy. After a moment or so she would pick it up gently in her mouth, carry it back to the hutch and then reappear with another one. This performance would be repeated until I had had every puppy in my lap; then she was satisfied and would let me get on with my work.

It is hard to know what a large percentage of the human race would do without these incredibly tough and reliable members of the dog family. They do, after all, enable man to exist in a portion of the globe where he would be hard pressed if it were not for the help of the husky. A Dr. Guillemard, writing in the 1800s, describes the huskies he saw in Camp Kamchatka as follows.

Most of them are white, with black heads, or entirely of a brown black; and their general aspect, owing to the sharp muzzle and prick ears, is decidedly wolf-like. The only food they are provided with by their masters is salmon of the hump-backed kind; but during the summer they pick up game, eggs, and birds in their wanderings about the country. They are usually inspanned in teams of eight or ten, but where the sledges are heavy or the roads bad, double that number, or

even more are occasionally used. When the snow is hard and
even, they will draw a weight of 360 lbs. a distance of five-
and-thirty or forty miles with ease in a day's work; and with
an unloaded sledge, with a single occupant, a pace of eight
versts an hour can be kept up for a considerable time. On the
road they are given one-third of a fish twice during the day,
and a fish and a half at night, which they wash down with a
few gulps of snow. . . . Each has a name, which he answers
to when he is driven in the sledge, just in the same way as a
Cape ox in a waggon team, for no whips are used. If chas-
tisement be necessary, the driver throws his stick at the
delinquent, or pounds the unfortunate creature with any stone
that comes handy. There are many ways of tethering these
animals, all having in view the one object of keeping them
apart, as, excepting upon the road, they seize every opportunity of fighting. One method is by making a large tripod of
poles, and tying a dog at the bottom of each; and in many
villages, owing to the large number of dogs which have to be
kept, these tripods form a characteristic feature.

The huskies in my charge displayed incredible strength and
were completely oblivious to the weather. They used their
wooden hutches only for having their puppies in and much
preferred, even in heavy snow, to dig a hole for themselves
and sleep out. They also displayed a completely catholic taste
in food that would have done credit to an ostrich. One of
them ate a handkerchief one day; such things as bus tickets
or ice-cream cartons pushed through the wire by the animal-
loving British public were immediately engulfed with apparent enjoyment; and one day, whilst I was sweeping out one
of the paddocks, I dropped my wallet—fortunately empty—
and in two gulps it had disappeared down the throat of one
of the young dogs, who seemed delighted at this largesse and

suffered no ill effects from it; so it came as no surprise to me to read Dr. Guillemard's comments on the husky's fortitude.

> No comfortable home is provided for him to enable him to withstand the rigours of the Arctic climate, and the poor beast, except when actually at work, has, in most cases, to "find himself." Long experience, and the instinct transmitted to him by his ancestors have, however, given him all the resources of an old campaigner. Stumbling at night about the uncertain paths of the settlements, the traveller is not unfrequently precipitated into the huge rabbit-burrows which the animal constructs to avoid the cutting winds. His coat, nearly as thick as that of a bear, is composed of fur rather than hair. . . . Wonderfully well-trained, cunning and enduring, he is at the same time often obstinate and unmanageable to a degree, and is apparently indifferent to the kicks and blows so liberally showered upon him by his master. Excepting in settlements where neighbouring stretches of tundra render the use of sledges possible in summer, he has a long holiday during that season. During this time he wanders over the country at will, sometimes returning at night to his burrow, at others being absent for days together. A good hunter and fisherman, he supports himself upon the game and salmon he catches, and it is but rarely that he deserts his master for good. But the inhabitants have to pay a good price for his services. Owing to his rapacity it is impossible to keep sheep, goats, or any of the smaller domestic animals, and Kamschatka is one of the few countries in the world in which fowls are unknown.

Wandering freely about in the park were, as well as the wallabies and the peacocks, the diminutive little antelopes called muntjaks and a lot of Chinese water deer. These very curious deer were about the size of an airedale, and you would think that in a large paddock where the turf had been cropped down by various herds of antelopes and deer an animal this size would be conspicuous; but a Chinese water deer lying down in grass three inches long just seems to melt away and you do not see it until you have almost stepped on it. They are a dull shade of yellow-brown, and the hair is rather coarse. When you look at the individual hairs closely you will see that each one is slightly flattened and jointed, like a miniature piece of bamboo. These odd deer do not grow horns, but instead, in the male, the canine teeth are elongated into two Dracula-like tusks which the males use in fighting for possession of the females and probably, in parts of their range, to dig in the snow for roots and bulbs.

I received news one morning that one of these deer, filled with the spirit of adventure or a migrating urge, had somehow made his escape through the perimeter fence that surrounded the whole of the park and had managed to find his way into a local field which was fenced in as a chicken run. Phil Bates, myself and Billy, who happened to be doing nothing at the time, went down to recapture the truant. We took a little green van stuffed with nets and drove down to the field, which covered about a quarter of an acre and was shaped like an isosceles triangle.

In the center of it stood the Chinese water deer, surrounded by a group of excited and interested chickens; he looked as though he were just giving them a lecture on the beauties of travel. He gave a start of horror when he saw us entering the field and, metaphorically, lost his place in his notes. He looked rather like a parliamentary candidate who perceives with nervousness that a rowdy element is creeping into his audience.

We spread the pig nets out in order to cut down the area over which we would have to chase him, and he watched us with ever-increasing alarm. The idea was for two of us to

chivvy him round so that he became entangled in the pig nets
while the third person stood by to leap in and subdue him at the
right moment. There was only one flaw in our plans, and that
was that he refused to be entangled in the nets. Pursued by
us, he ran round and round the field but always adroitly managed to change course so that he came nowhere near the nets.
We had a hasty consultation and decided that we would try
the rugger-tackle plan. The chickens hitherto had been a
deeply fascinated but orderly group of spectators, but this
proved too much for them. As the first of us landed with a
resounding thump in the grass some four yards behind the
deer's tail, the chickens broke ranks. The air was full of cries
of pain from winded and bruised hunters, shrill startled
squawks from the chickens, and clouds of feathers.

The Chinese water deer became more and more panic-
stricken and started hurling himself at the tall wire fence in
an effort to break through. He made one prodigious leap, hit
the fence and hooked himself neatly onto the mesh by his two
tusks and hung there kicking and struggling. We made a
concerted rush, but at the last minute he managed to unhook
himself with a magnificent display of muscular contraction
and, landing on the grass, turned with tremendous speed and
broke through our ranks. He passed close by me, and so,
fixing my eye firmly on his hind leg, I launched myself through
the air with what I hoped was hawklike grace. The next three
seconds were confused and painful. I got an iron grip on his
leg and we rolled over and over together into what turned out
to be the only patch of thistles and nettles in the whole field.
The deer lashed out with his free hind leg, and his hoofs, as
sharp as a knife, slashed me neatly from wrist to elbow. We
rolled over and over together and I still managed to maintain

my grip on his leg in spite of the fact that he had turned his head and I felt his tusks slash the back of my hand.

But this was his final gesture of defiance; suddenly, he stopped struggling altogether and started to give vent to the most bloodcurdling and piercing screams. He could not have produced a better performance if I had been burning him with a red-hot iron. As it was, I was quite shaken and relaxed my grip considerably, under the impression that I was hurting him, but as we were pushing him carefully into a sack Phil explained that this was the normal way a Chinese water deer accepted his fate.

He lay in the sack, still uttering these ear-splitting screams, while we collected up the nets. Then we put him into the van on top of them and started to drive back to the park. I felt sure that the novelty of driving in the van would make the animal stop, but not a bit of it. We were forced to drive the entire length of the park with these fearsome screams issuing forth from the back of the van without pause. Each person we passed went pale and looked after the van with the horrified expression that they would have assumed had the driver been headless. One stout, military-looking man stopped dead and glared after us as though he were half contemplating giving chase and demanding to see our vivisection license. The deer continued to scream unremittingly until we reached the area we were to release him in. Pig killing was music in comparison to the noise that this comparatively small animal produced. Eventually, we shook him out of the sack and he stopped screaming. Then two quick bounds and he crouched down in the grass and disappeared.

One day I noticed that one of my foxes had developed a type of boil at the base of its tail. I went to Phil with the news and he procured for me from Captain Beale some ointment with which I had to anoint the boil every day. This was a tedious performance and one that the fox, being highly nervous, did not enjoy, for it meant that he had to be caught up. I did the catching with something resembling a large butterfly net. It had a heavy metal rim padded rather ineffectually with sacking, and the bag was made out of coarse fishing net. The actual catching process was fairly easy, owing to the fox's set pattern of behavior. As soon as he was routed out of his den and the door to it closed, he would start to run round and round the outer perimeter of the cage at a steady canter. All that was needed was to place the net suddenly and swiftly just in front of him and, provided it was close enough to him, he would run straight into it. One had to be careful, however, for the metal rim, although padded, could be dangerous.

On the fourth day the boil was showing distinct signs of improvement when I went to catch up the fox. He was circling the perimeter of the cage and I was edging the net into position when Billy rode up on his bicycle. I did not notice him and so just as I swept the net forward I was startled by Billy suddenly shouting "Yoo hoo!" in a falsetto screech through the wire. In my surprise I raised the net a fatal two inches, so that the fox, instead of running into the bag, was caught across his forelegs by the metal rim. There was a noise like a rotten twig breaking as the fox's right foreleg snapped neatly, halfway between elbow and paw.

"You bloody idiot!" I said to Billy. "Look what you've made me do."

"I'm sorry," said Billy contritely, staring at the fox, which was still circling the cage with undiminished speed on three legs. "I didn't see what you were doing."

"It's Phil's day off, too," I said, "so what the hell am I supposed to do? I can't leave it like this."

"Take it to Daddy," said Bill promptly. "Take it to Daddy and he'll set it. That's what Phil would do."

I suddenly remembered that the captain was a qualified veterinary surgeon, and so this seemed intelligent advice.

"Where is your father?" I asked.

"In the office," said Billy. "He's in the office working. He says he always works better on a Saturday, when there are no secretaries and things to disturb him."

"Right," I said. "Well, we'll go and disturb him."

I caught the fox and extricated it, snapping and snarling, from the net. For their size silver foxes can put up a show of ferocity that would be envied by a Bengal tiger. On examination I found that the break was a beautiful one; that is to say that if a broken leg *can* be beautiful, this one was, for the bone was not splintered into a compound or squashed and bent into a green-stick fracture. It was a lovely clean break, as neat as snapping a stick of celery. Of course I did not expect the fox to share my enthusiasm, but I knew such a clean break would be much easier to set and would stand a better chance of healing successfully.

When we got to the administration block we found that the captain had finished his desk work and had retired to his house for a bath. Having acquired this knowledge from Mrs. Beale, I would have been content to wait until the captain had finished his ablutions. However, both Mrs. Beale and Billy said that the length of time that the captain spent in the bath was unpredictable and so, on humanitarian grounds, he ought to be disturbed. Billy went and battered on the bathroom door.

"Go 'way!" roared the captain, making noises like fourteen frightened hippos trying to extricate themselves from a garden pond. "Go 'way. I'm bathing."

"Hurry up," shouted Billy. "Weve got a fox with a broken leg."

There was a pause and one could hear the water lapping softly.

"What d'you say?" asked the captain suspiciously.

"A fox with a broken leg," repeated Billy.

"No peaçe!" roared the captain. "There's no peace in this place. All right—put it in the office and I'll be there."

So we went into the captain's office and waited. We could hear the captain clearly.

"Gladys! *Gladys!* Where are my slippers? Oh, it's all right, they're here. They've brought in a fox with a broken leg. Get that new plaster bandage ready. . . . Well, how do *I* know

230

where it is? Look for it. It must be somewhere. And, Gladys, where are my underpants?"

Eventually, rosy from his bath, he lumbered into the office, followed by Mrs. Beale carrying a huge tin.

"Ah, Durrell, it's you, heh?" he rumbled. "A fox, heh? Let's have a look."

The fox, who had more or less accepted his fate and was lying quiescent in my arms, was alarmed at Captain Beale's size, proximity and rich voice. It opened its mouth and gave a long, warning, yarring snarl. The captain stepped back hurriedly.

"Hold it," he barked at me. "Get a good grip on its neck."

"I have, Captain," I pointed out.

Short of decapitating the poor animal I could not have held it more firmly.

I slid my hand gently under the broken leg and lifted it slightly so that the captain could see the extent of the damage.

"Heh," he said, straightening his spectacles and peering. "Nice clean break. That's something. Now to work. Billy, get me scissors."

"Where do I find scissors?" inquired Billy helplessly.

"Where the hell do you think?" snarled the captain. "Use your head! In your mother's workbasket, of course."

Billy disappeared in search of scissors.

"And tell Laura we want her," shouted the captain. "We need all the help we can get."

I gazed at the slender, diminutive creature in my arms and wondered what the captain's reaction would have been if it had been something bigger—a blackbuck or a giraffe, for example.

"Laura's doing her homework," said Mrs. Beale "Can't we manage, dear?"

"No," said the captain decisively, taking the tin from her hands. "This is new stuff. I need help."

"But I'm helping, dear."

"I need everybody's help," said the captain austerely.

Billy returned with the scissors and his sister.

"Now," said the captain oratorically, sticking a thumb under his braces, "this is what we've got to do. First, we cut the hair off the leg, understand?"

"Why?" asked Billy, obtusely.

"Because the bloody plaster won't stick on hair," said the captain, exasperated by such lack of perception.

"Don't shout, William—you're frightening the fox," said Mrs. Beale anxiously.

"If you're all going to argue, can I go back and finish my homework?" inquired Laura.

"You stay here," snapped the captain. "You might be a vital link in the chain."

"Yes, Daddy."

"Now, Durrell," said the captain, "this plaster bandage is new stuff, y'see?"

He slapped the tin with his hand, and a pale cloud of plaster of Paris puffed out and spread over his desk.

"Is it, sir?" I asked. I was genuinely interested.

"Yes," said the captain, hooking his thumbs back behind his braces. "In the old days, d'you see, you had to splint, bandage and then muck about with plaster of Paris. Messy. Took a long time."

I knew that it was time-consuming, messy and in a lot of ways unsuccessful, for I had used this method on more than one occasion for birds with broken wings and legs, but it was not for me to say so. Apart from anything else, it was obvious

232

that the captain was going to show me a modern method of splinting that would be quick, nonmessy and foolproof. This, after all, was what I had come to Whipsnade for—the acquisition of knowledge.

"Now," said the captain, "this is the modern method."

He lifted the tin and peered at it, shifting his glasses down to the end of his nose and drawing his mouth down in a sneer of disbelief.

"Rmm . . . rmm . . . rmm . . . umble . . . umble . . . umble," he murmured, reading to himself. "Yes, that's clear. Lukewarm water, Gladys. And now you, Billy, cut the hair off the leg."

"Can't I go back to my homework?" asked Laura plaintively.

"No," barked the captain. "You're to—to—to sweep up the hair off the floor. Hygiene."

The captain had now got us all at action stations and integrated. Mrs. Beale was clattering about in the kitchen producing the water, Billy and I were struggling in a fox-shearing contest that the fox took grave exception to, and Laura was mutinously sweeping the floor. Having thus deployed his forces, the captain took the lid off the tin and rather uneasily unraveled a yard or two of bandage heavily impregnated with plaster of Paris. He paced to and fro as he examined this with interest. Most of the plaster of Paris fell on the floor, making the office look as though it was suffering a light but clinging snowfall, while the finer particles of plaster floated in the air like a faint mist and made us all cough.

"What will they think of next?" marveled the captain to himself, spreading plaster of Paris like a hoarfrost as he paced up and down.

Mrs. Beale reappeared with a saucepan full of warm water.

"Good," said the captain, starting to organize. "Now, Billy, Laura, Gladys, get hold of this bandage."

In a cloud of plaster he unraveled some sixteen feet of bandage and handed it to his family.

"Hold it out straight," he commanded. "Out *straight*, Gladys! You're *drooping*. . . . That's right. You ready, Durrell?"

"Yes, sir," I said.

"Got a good grip on its neck, heh? Don't want it breaking loose at the crucial moment."

"Yes, sir, I've got it tight."

"Good," said the captain, and, seizing the saucepan, he made his way down the length of bandage, slopping water on it. "D'you see how it works, Durrell?" he asked, seizing the dripping end of the bandage and waving it at me. "No more splints, d'you see? The bandage acts as a splint."

He wound several inches of the bandage round his forefinger to demonstrate.

"No mucking about with splints," he said, wagging his finger at me. "None of the old-fashioned mess, d'you see?"

The captain's desk and the floor of the office looked like a badly concocted ski slope, but it was not for me to point it out.

It was at this moment that things started to become confused. Whether the captain had misread the instructions I am not sure, but the bandage round his finger solidified with astonishing rapidity and firmness.

"Bloody hell," said the captain vehemently.

"William, dear!"

"Where are the scissors? Who's taken the blasted scissors?"

The scissors were found and the captain cut himself loose from the tenacious bandage. During the process he got a considerable quantity of plaster smeared on his spectacles.

"Now, Durrell," he said, squinting owlishly at the fox, "hold its leg out."

Dutifully I held its leg out and the captain wound several turns of bandage round the break, slopping more water about as he did so. The fox, Captain Beale and I all started to look distinctly aquatic.

"More bandage!" rumbled the captain, intent on his work.

It was then that another snag made itself apparent. Without constant moistening, the length of bandage held by Mrs. Beale, Laura and Billy had solidified, sticking firmly to their hands and linking them together like a daisy chain.

"You're all bloody useless," shouted the captain as he cut them loose. "You're supposed to *help!* Now unwind some more bandage."

Billy, in an effort to assuage his father's wrath, knocked the tin onto the floor, and it rolled across the office, shedding bandage and plaster of Paris in equal quantities. The place was begining to look like an advanced casualty station in one of the fiercer Napoleonic battles. Everyone and everything appeared to be covered in a fine layer of plaster and loops of bandage.

"*Useless!*" roared the captain. "Bloody useless, the lot of you! Look at you all—look at the bandage. You're all a lot of—a lot of—a lot of nincompoops!"

At length the captain was calmed down by Mrs. Beale, and then while Laura and Billy unraveled some more bandage

Mrs. Beale moistened it, and the captain, his face still puce-colored, his breathing stertorous, wound it round the fox's leg. A last he stood back.

"That should do," he said.

It was not the most professional piece of splinting I had ever seen, but the captain seemed satisfied. He stood there beaming, his glasses covered with a white rim of plaster, his bald head as white as though powdered, bits of bandage solidified on his clothing, and a long strip wound inextricably round his slipper.

"There you are, Durrell," he rumbled in a self-satisfied way. These modern things make all the difference to the job—simplify things, d'you see?"

"Yes, sir," I said.

CHAPTER 10

Beasts in My Belfry

———◆———

*Some beasts be ordained for man's
mirth, as apes and marmosets and pop-
injays; and some be made for exercita-
tion of man, for man should know his
own infirmities and the might of God.
And therefore be made flies and lice;
and lions and tigers and bears be made
that man may by the first know his own
infirmity, and be afeard of the second.
Also some beasts be made to relieve and
help the need of many manner infirmities of mankind—as the flesh of the
adder to make treacle.*
    —BARTHOLOMEW THE ENGLISHMAN,
        De proprietatibus rerum

I HAD been at Whipsnade a little over a year when I decided to leave. This was no hasty decision; I was still as determined as ever to go animal collecting and eventually to own my own zoo, but I knew that I would not be hastening the achievement of either ambition by staying any longer at Whipsnade. I could have stayed on indefinitely being odd-beast boy, but I had other plans.

On my twenty-first birthday, a date that was not too far distant, I knew I was to inherit three thousand pounds—not a fortune, but in those days one could do a lot more with three thousand than one can today. So every evening in the cold, echoing confines of the Bothy I would sit in my little cell-like room and write carefully composed letters to all the animal collectors who were then functioning. I outlined my experience and then went on to say that if they would consider taking me on an expedition I would pay all my own expenses and work free. Eventually, back came the replies, courteous but definite. They appreciated my offer but as I had had no collecting experience it was impossible for them to consider taking

me on a trip; if I could get some collecting experience, however, I was to approach them again. As my whole reason for
wanting to go on an expedition was to gain experience, this
argument was, to say the least, unhelpful. It was the egg and
the chicken all over again: they would not take me unless I
had the experience, and I could not get the experience unless
they took me.

It was at that point in my life, depressed and frustrated,
that I had a brilliant idea. If I used some of my inheritance to
finance an expedition of my own, then I could honestly claim
to have had experience and then one of these great men might
not only take me on an expedition but actually pay me a salary.
The prospects were mouth-watering.

My desire to leave was greeted with disappointment. Phil
Bates tried to persuade me to stay on, as did Captain Beale.

"You'll never get anywhere, Durrell, if you keep leaving
like this," he grumbled aggrievedly at my farewell curry
supper, as if I had made a habit of giving in my notice once a
week during my time at Whipsnade. "You should stay on.
Give you a section of your own eventually. Could lead to big
things."

"It's very kind of you, sir, but I've got my heart set on
going collecting."

"No money in it," said the captain dolefully. "You'll be
chuckin' money away, mark my words."

"Don't depress the boy, William," said Mrs. Beale. "I'm
sure he'll make a success of it."

"Fiddy faddy!" said the captain glumly. "Nobody ever
made money collecting."

"What about Hagenbeck, sir?" I inquired.

"Those were the good old days," said the captain. "Money

was money then—gold sovereigns you could dig your teeth into, not a lot of useless lavatory paper like we've got now."

"William, dear!"

"Well, it's true, said the captain truculently. "In those days money was worth money. Now it's a lot of loo paper."

"William!"

"Anyway, come back and see us, won't you?" said the captain.

"Yes, you must," said Mrs. Beale. "We shall miss you."

"I'll earmark all the best animals in my collection for you, sir," I said.

As I lay in bed on my last night at Whipsnade I tried to assess how important my being there had been to me. What had I learned?

It seemed to be mostly negative. True, I had learned the best way to carry a bale of hay on a pitchfork, how to use a besom and spade for cleaning out, and the fact that a docile-looking wallaby could, when cornered, jump at you, slash down with its hind feet and rip the front off an extremely tough mackintosh; but it seemed that it was the how-not-to I had learned that was important.

I had come to realize that one of the most vital things in a zoological garden is the keepering staff. Without them nothing is achieved, so therefore it is of the utmost importance to give status to a hard and dirty job and, what is more important, to pick these people carefully. The keepering staff at Whipsnade when I was there were, in the main, farm laborers who had been employed originally to put up the great perimeter fence and the paddock fencing. The result was that I found myself working with men of forty and fifty who did not know as much about the animals in their care as I did at twenty. This was not their fault; they had no desire to be zoological experts. As far as they were concerned it was just a job of work, and they did it as efficiently as they could but with an almost total lack of interest. This was brought home to me very forcibly my first day on the giraffe section.

At about four o'clock Bert had instructed me to light a fire under a great caldron of water, and this I had dutifully done. When it was boiling he carefully mixed hot and cold water together to make a couple of buckets of tepid water and then told me that we were going to give the giraffe his drink. As I watched the giraffe gulping down the water I asked Bert why it was necessary for its drinking water to be warm.

"Dunno, boy," said Bert. "When 'e came they told me to give 'im 'ot water—dunno why."

Careful inquiry on my part solved the mystery. Six or seven years before, when the giraffe had first arrived, it had developed a chill; it was thought that warm water would be more soothing to drink than cold, and so instructions were given— but never countermanded. The result was that the giraffe had been drinking hot water for seven years quite unnecessarily. Bert, who was very fond and proud of his animals, had nevertheless lacked sufficient interest to find out if warm water was essential to the giraffe's welfare.

Lack of interest or lack of knowledge breeds lack of observation, and of all the qualifications needed when looking after wild animals this is the most important. Wild animals are past masters at concealing the fact that they are ill, for example, so that unless you know your creatures intimately and observe them most carefully you will miss the tiny signs that tell you the creature is unwell.

Another point which became very obvious to me at Whipsnade was the totally erroneous idea that an animal was happier and therefore lived better in a larger cage or enclosure than a small one. "I don't mind zoos if they're like Whipsnade," was the remark that was so frequently made by those well-meaning and ignorant animal lovers that I met. The answer was, of course, "You should have worked there—and experienced the difficulty of trying to keep a close daily check on a herd of animals in a thirty-five-acre paddock, making sure they were developing no illness, that some of them were not being bullied to starvation level by the others, and that the whole group was getting enough to eat."

If anything went wrong and you had to catch up an individual member of the herd, you would have to pursue it round thirty-five acres and when you had finally caught it— you hoped, without its dying of heart failure or breaking a leg—you had to treat it not only for whatever was wrong with it but for acute shock as well. Nowadays, of course, things are made much easier by the use of such refinements as dart guns, but in the days when I worked at Whipsnade the size of the paddock was ultimately detrimental to the animals. The only useful function they fulfilled was as a salve to the anthropomorphic souls of those animal lovers who did not like to see animals "imprisoned." Unfortunately, this attitude toward zoos is still rife among the well-intentioned but basically ignorant who still insist on talking about Mother Nature as though she were a benevolent old lady instead of the harsh, unyielding and totally rapacious monster that she is.

It is hard to argue with these people; they live in a euphoric state where they believe that an animal in a zoo suffers as though it were in Dartmoor and an animal in its natural surroundings is living in a Garden of Eden where the lamb can lie down with the lion without starting in friendship and ending up as dinner. It is useless pointing out the ceaseless drudgery of finding adequate food supplies each day in the wilds, of the constant strain on the nerves of avoiding enemies, of the battle against disease and parasites, of the fact that in some species there is more than a fifty percent mortality rate among their young in the first six months. "Ah," these bemused animal lovers will say when these things are pointed out to them, "but they are *free*." You point out that animals have strict territories that are governed by three things: food, water and sex. Provide all these successfully within a limited area and the animal will stay there. But people seem to be obsessed with this word "freedom," particularly when applied to animals. They never seen to worry about the freedom of the bank clerks of Streatham, the miners of Durham, the factory hands of Sheffield, the carpenters of Hartley Wintney, or the headwaiters of Soho, yet if a careful survey were conducted on these and other similar species you would find that they are as confined by their jobs and by convention as securely as any zoo inmate.

The following morning I went the rounds saying goodbye to the animals and men. I was sad, for I had been happy working at Whipsnade but as I went round, each animal represented a place I wanted to see, each was a sort of geographical signpost encouraging me on my way. Peter the Wombat, noisily devouring a final bag of peanuts from me, represented the topsy-turvy continent of Australia with its strange red deserts and its stranger fauna, a fauna that leaped and bounced, mammals that laid eggs like birds, and similar wonders that I must witness. The tigers Paul and Maurena, accepting a farewell egg, their hides glowing a sunset-orange, were Asia—bejeweled elephants, great armored rhinoceroses, and the gleaming, bespangled ramparts of the Himalayas alive with wild sheep. Babs and Sam the polar bears, hissing delightedly over their ice creams, spoke to me of jagged milk-white snow fields and a deep, cold sea as blue and as uncomforting as a crow's wing. The dazzling black-and-white zebras and old Albert wrapped in his tangled mane were Africa, the dark continent, its shiny green and moist forests sheltering the massive gorilla, its savannas shaking under the impact of a million galloping hoofs, its lakes a rose garden of pink flamingoes.

Everywhere, the animals beckoned me and strengthened my decision. As I stuffed bananas under the rubbery noses of the tapirs and slapped their fat rumps for the last time, I thought of visiting their South American homeland—huge trees bejeweled with spritelike marmosets, and great slow rivers, coffee-brown, their waters full of razor-toothed fish and placid turtles. There were so many places to go and so many animals to see that I was flooded with impatience. The brown bears and the wolves represented the whispering northern forests; Peter the giraffe, in his latticework coat, beckoned me to the fawn-colored plains of Africa, grass as crisp as a biscuit underfoot, shaded by the strange topiary of acacias, while the shaggy-shouldered buffalo lured me to the great sweeping undulations of the North American prairies.

The men I had worked with took my news in various ways. "Remember what I learnt you, boy," said Jesse, sucking his teeth and blaring at me. "And watch out. It's one thing to have a lion in a cage and another to have the bugger creeping up behind you, see? You watch it, boy."

"I don't know how you can do it," said Joe, pursing his lips and shaking his head. "I couldn't—not if you was to offer me a hundred pounds I couldn't. But do as Jesse says and watch it."

"Off to Africa are we?" said Mr. Cole. "Quite the little explorer then."

"Goodbye, boy," said old Tom, enveloping my hand in both his fat, red, chilblain-encrusted ones and squeezing it. "Send us a postcard, won't you? Take care of yourself."

"Good luck, boy," said Harry, his eyes twinkling. "Not that you need it—I know you'll be all right. Why, you can run near as fast as I can when anything comes for you. You'll be OK."

"Goodbye, lad," said Bert, ducking under the giraffe's great neck to shake my hand, adding, as though I were getting married, "I hope you'll be very happy."

"If you want any help, just drop us a line," said Phil Bates, his brown face earnest. "I'm sure the captain will always help you, and if you ever want to come back, well, I'm sure we can manage something."

He beamed at me, shook my hand, and then wandered off whistling tunelessly through the green woods asparkle with a treasure of daffodils, the wallabies and the peacocks moving slowly, unconcernedly, out of his way.

I picked up my suitcase and made my way out of the park.

Epilogue

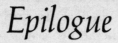

ONE thing Whipsnade did do for me: it made me an even more avid and omnivorous reader than I was already. Here I was surrounded by a thousand questions and I was also surrounded by people who could not answer them, so I had to resort to books. I discovered, rather to my surprise, that zoological gardens were not a modern innovation. King Solomon, for example, had a zoo in 794 B.C. and, earlier than that, in 2900 B.C., zoological gardens were flourishing in Saqqara in Egypt. Thutmose III had a zoo in 1501 B.C., and his stepmother, Hatshepsut (admirable woman that she must have been), actually sent animal-collecting expeditions to the land of Punt (now Somaliland). Ramses II had an enviable collection which boasted, among other things, giraffes. After these notable zoo owners, the Chinese started and the Emperor Wen Wang established a 1,500-acre park which he called Ling-yu, or Garden of Intelligence, an appropriate name for a zoo if it is run and used properly. The Assyrians had many zoos, owned by such people as Semiramis, courtesan of the Assyrian court (who was a leopard fancier), her son Ninus (who fancied lions), and King Ashurbanipal, whose expertise lay in lions and camels. Ptolemy I founded a huge zoo in Alexandria, and this was continued and enlarged by Ptolemy II. An indication of its scope was a procession held on the Feast of Dionysus which took all day to pass the stadium in Alexandria and included, amongst other things, eight pairs of ostriches in harness, peacocks, guinea fowl, pheasants, no fewer than ninety-six elephants, twenty-four lions, fourteen leopards, sixteen pantharoi or cheetahs, six pairs of dromedaries, a giraffe, a huge snake, and a rhinoceros, in addition to hundreds of domestic animals. Most modern zoos would be hard pressed to produce such a display.

The first European zoos were Greek and Roman, and these were kept partly as study areas, partly as adjuncts of the circus. Up to Victorian times zoological gardens fulfilled two functions: they allowed the closer study of animals and they provided what was considered an edifying and amusing spectacle of God's wonders for his next of kin, man. Unfortunately, zoological gardens gradually became places of amusement first and places of scientific advancement a very poor second, except for a few notable exceptions. Animals were merely kept to amuse the public; people went to the zoo in the same spirit that their ancestors used to visit Bedlam. Unfortunately, today many people still visit the zoo in the same spirit, but interest in the behavior and ecology of animals is growing and this is a healthy sign. In the old days, when the world seemed a bottomless cornucopia stuffed with animal life, it was perhaps understandable that a zoological collection was merely an interesting sideshow and nothing more. For example, no really serious attempt was made to breed the animals that were kept; if they died they were simply replaced—from what seemed like Mother Nature's endless store. Today this seems unforgivable.

As I pursued my reading I began to learn with horror of man's rapacious encroachment upon the world and the terrible devastation that he was producing among animal life. I read of the dodo, flightless and harmless, discovered and exterminated almost in the same breath. I read of the passenger pigeons in North America, whose vast numbers "darkened the sky," who were so numerous that their nesting colonies measured several hundred square miles. They were good to eat; the last one died in the Cincinnati Zoo in 1914. The last quagga, that strange half horse, half zebra once so common in South Africa, was harried to extinction by the Boer farmers; the last quagga died in the London Zoo in 1909. It seemed incredible, almost impossible, that people in charge of zoos should have been so ignorant that they did not realize that these animals and birds were tottering on the border of extinction and that they did not do something about it. Surely this was one of the true functions of a zoological garden, to help animals that were being pushed toward extinction? Why hadn't they done this? It was because, I think, in those days they worked on the principle of "there's plenty more where that came from." But the world is dwindling, the numbers of mankind are ever increasing, and more and more we are discovering that there is not "plenty more where that came from."

When I left Whipsnade, I was still determined to have a zoo of my own, but I was equally determined that if I ever achieved this ambition my zoo would have to fulfill three functions in order to justify its existence. Firstly, it would have to act as an aid to the education of people so that they would realize how fascinating and how important the other forms of life in the world were, so that they would stop being quite so arrogant and self-important and appreciate the fact that the other forms of life had just as much right to existence as they had. Secondly, research into the behavior of animals would be undertaken so that by this means one could not only learn more about the behavior of human beings but also be in a better position to help animals in their wild state, for unless you know the needs of the various species of animal you cannot practice conservation successfully. Thirdly—and this seemed to me to be of the utmost urgency—the zoo would have to be a reservoir of animal life, a sanctuary for threatened species, keeping and breeding them so that they would not vanish from the earth forever as the dodo, the quagga and the passenger pigeon had done.

For many years after leaving Whipsnade I was lucky enough to be able to undertake expeditions to various parts of the world collecting animals, and during these trips I became increasingly aware of the dangers that threatened animal life: the direct danger of the actual killing of the animal and the indirect danger of the destruction of its habitat. It seemed to me that the establishment of a breeding sanctuary for an ever-increasing number of threatened species was of the utmost urgency. So I founded my own zoological park in Jersey in the Channel Islands and presently I created the Jersey Wildlife Preservation Trust, which took over the park as its headquarters.

To describe the aims and objects of this trust I can do no better than to quote from a brochure I wrote about our activities.

Although in recent years there has been a great awakening of interest in the conservation of animal life and its habitat, the process of protection is a slow one. In a great many countries although the animals are officially protected, this is "paper protection" only, since the governments or the wildlife departments concerned have not as yet the money or the manpower to implement the law completely. All over the world innumerable species are threatened by the direct or indirect intervention of man. It must be remembered that it is just as easy to eliminate a numerous species by destroying or altering its habitat as it is by indiscriminate slaughter with guns.

In many cases the population of a certain creature has dropped so low that it can no longer hope to survive unaided, for its numbers are too small for it to be able to cope with the natural hazards of existence, i.e. predators, or perhaps a failing food supply. It is these species that the Trust is concentrating on. If breeding colonies of these can be set up in ideal surroundings, with an unlimited food supply, freedom from predators, and their offspring guarded from the moment they are born, then these species will survive. At a later date when, in their countries of origin, sufficient funds are available for adequate conservation measures to be put into operation, then a nucleus breeding stock from the Trust's collection can be returned to re-populate those areas in which the species has become extinct.

That this is not only possible but a very necessary course of action has been proved on numerous occasions. The Père David's Deer, for example, became extinct in China but, due to the late Duke of Bedford, a breeding colony was built up at Woburn Abbey. This magnificent deer is now safe and recently it has been re-introduced to China.

Another spectacular example of this type of work was the saving of the Hawaiian Goose from extinction by Peter Scott's Wildfowl Trust. Due to Mr. Scott's efforts, large breeding colonies have been established in various zoological and avicultural institutions throughout the world, the bird has been re-introduced to Hawaii and is now spreading over its former range.

The list of such successes is a long one, including such creatures as the European Bison, Przewalski's Wild Horse, the Saiga Antelope, and so on.

It will therefore be seen that the Jersey Wildlife Preservation Trust is a form of stationary Noah's Ark. Its intention is merely to try and save certain species from total eradication in exactly the same way that a museum provides protection for great works of art and various societies provide protection for ancient monuments and buildings. The animals that share the planet with us are just as important and, while it is conceivable that another Rembrandt or Leonardo da Vinci might be born, once an animal species is exterminated no amount of effort on our part—even in this age of frightening technology—can reproduce it again.

If you who have read this book have enjoyed it, then may I ask you to join me in my efforts to save some species of animal life from extinction?

Will you join my trust? The annual subscription is small, but I can assure you that your money is put to good purpose. If you are interested in the fate of animal life please write to me for details at

> Jersey Wildlife Preservation Trust
> Les Augres Manor
> Jersey
> Channel Islands.

From the point of view of the animals this work is of the utmost urgency, so please join me.

Bibliography

The Animal-Lore of Shakespeare's Time, Emma Phipson; Kegan Paul, Trench & Co., London, 1833

The Book of Beasts, T. H. White (Ed.); Jonathan Cape, London, 1954

The Encyclopedia of Witchcraft and Demonology, Rossell Hope Robbins; Peter Nevil, London, 1958

The History of Four-Footed Beasts and Serpents, Edward Topsel; London MDCLVIII

The Royal Natural History, Richard Lydekker (Ed.); Frederick Warne & Co., London, 1894

Vanishing Animals, Philip Street; Faber & Faber, London

Red Data Books: Aves & Mammalia; International Union for the Conservation of Nature and Natural Resources, Morges, Switzerland.

Pliny, Purchas and Elpis are other sources referred to.